Encounters with Bob Dylan

If You See Him, Say Hello

Tracy Johnson

humble press

San Francisco

For my parents, Darroll and Barbara Johnson, with gratitude.
Their encouragement and love have been a life raft at the lowest points.

Cover photo by Rowland Scherman (Newport, 1963)

Editing and design by Jon Sievert

Quotes from Bob Dylan lyrics used with permission

Cataloging-in-Publication Data

Johnson, Tracy
      Encounters with Bob Dylan/Tracy Johnson—1st ed.
            p.   cm.

1. Dylan, Bob, 1941–
2. Rock Musicians—United States—Biography

782.42162—dc21
ML420.D98J655 2000   LCCN: 99–068759
ISBN: 0-9647009-2-1

Printed in the United States of America.

humble press
P. O. Box 4322
Daly City, CA 94016
(415) 469-8901
www.humblepress.com

03 02 01 00   5 4 3 2 1

Table of Contents

Foreword

Derek Barker *is the founder and editor of* ISIS, *the world-renowned Bob Dylan fanzine started in 1985. He lives with his wife Tracy, two stepchildren, and two cats in central England.*

In England, a "twitcher" is a bird watcher whose main interest is observing, and ticking off his or her list, as many rare species as possible. He or she may travel to Scotland to see an osprey or golden eagle. A more fanatical twitcher will journey anywhere in the country on the strength of a news report that a species not native to the UK has been blown to these shores by prevailing winds. This could be a Siberian thrush, or a rare North American visitor, such as the American robin.

The British music press reported the imminent arrival of another rare North American visitor in Spring 1978: singer/songwriter/musician/legend Bob Dylan. At the time, I was not only an enthusiastic music lover, but an avid concert-goer with more than a little of that twitcher instinct. Starting in the early 1970s, I attended hundreds of concerts, sometimes as many as five a week. Over the years, I managed to tick almost all the rare and famous names off my list.

I'd never seen the Beatles live, and guessed I never would. Hendrix left us in 1970, and Elvis Aaron Presley threw off his mortal coil just six months before the start of this, Dylan's mammoth 1978 world tour. Dylan had last visited mainland Britain in 1966, when I was 12. I liked his music and even owned a few albums—*Blonde on Blonde, Blood on the Tracks, Desire, Greatest Hits Volume II.* This surely would be my only chance to see Dylan in concert and tick him off my list.

Finally, the day arrived—Tuesday, June 20, 1978. The venue was Earls Court, London, and front-row seats were luckily the order of the day. We talked casually until the house lights dimmed and the big backing band (eleven musicians, including three female singers) came on. Following an instrumental warm-up tune, Dylan took a British stage for the first time in a dozen years. The greatest lyricsmith of our time opened with "Love Her with a Feeling," a cover version of a Tampa Red song. That was my first experience with the perversity of Bob Dylan.

As the concert continued, I became completely captivated. To this day, I'm uncertain how to define the word charisma, but whatever it is, Dylan has it in truckloads. To say that concert changed my life probably sounds somewhat melodramatic. Nonetheless, it's true. I came to Dylan's music late, but since that June evening 21 years ago, much of my life has been consumed by the man and his music. Even a large proportion of my close friends is from the Dylan fraternity.

I started the *ISIS* newsletter in September, 1985, to communicate with an ever-growing circle of friends. People sent snippets of Dylan news, which I collated and sent back out to all concerned. This "free" exchange of information continued for more than two years, until the sheer volume of participants and news made it impossible to continue in this vein. The five-page newsletter had grown to more than 30 pages and, by default, become a magazine. The only option left was to have it professionally printed with a cover price. The rest, as they say, is history.

Why have I devoted so much time listening to Dylan and running *ISIS*? Simple: I believe Bob Dylan is, without doubt, the most important songwriter of the 20th Century. Like so many fans, I've followed the numerous twists and turns of his extraordinary career with great interest. I continue in my endeavor because I believe he still has much to give. There are many in the mainstream music press who would have us believe that Dylan is a spent force creatively, a ghost from another era. It's therefore inspiring to receive so much mail from new young music fans focusing on Dylan as an artist. It's also refreshing that, after a rather barren recording period, 1998's *Time Out of Mind*, was received by critics with almost universal praise.

Over the years, the music industry has paid tribute to him with six Grammy awards and inauguration into the Rock and Roll Hall of Fame. In 1990, the French government awarded him the medal of "Commandeur des Arts et des Lettres," the highest cultural honor that can be bestowed on a non-national. More recently, The Kennedy Center Honors recognized Dylan's contributions with a "Lifetime Achievement Award," while the Gish Prize Trust presented him with their annual award given to "a man or woman who has made an outstanding contribution to the beauty of the world and to mankind's enjoyment and understanding of life."

I've often been asked if I'd like to meet Bob Dylan. The answer is *probably* not. To meet and talk with him may spoil the mystique that has cloaked his persona and captivated me for so many years. The closest I came was in 1987, at Wembley Arena, and it wasn't even that close. During Tom Petty's opening set, Dylan apparently came up from backstage to watch the show and sat down a couple of rows from me. I didn't even know he was there, but my friend Mark saw him from the main arena floor and futilely tried to signal me. Over the years, depending on how much beer has been consumed, Mark's tale of my close encounter has grown to one version that has Dylan sitting next to me and asking politely if I was enjoying the show. I make no retort, but move seats in the hope that this hooded vagrant will stop pestering me. Nevertheless, though I have never physically met the man, in a very real sense I encounter Bob Dylan virtually every day of my life.

I agreed to write the foreward to this book because it is unique. After so many important, but intense, analytical studies of Dylan and his lyrics, *Encounters with Bob Dylan* is like a breath of fresh air. For the first time, the people that really matter, the fans, are given a chance to tell their stories, give their thanks, and pay tribute to this remarkable man.

Preface

Tracy Johnson *is a freelance writer who lives in San Francisco. This is her first book. She compiled and edited these pieces over a period of two years.*

I t was on a rainy day in October, 1983, at the awkward age of 16, when I realized that Bob Dylan's words and music were fated to drastically alter my life.

I grew up with a military father and a family life that bore a striking resemblance to the film, *The Great Santini*. My folks couldn't have been more mismatched: a domineering and strict Air Force father and an artistic, dreamily emotional mother. Then again, their decision to tie the knot was like something out of a fiction novel anyway, having first encountered one another on the street back in 1962 and saying their "I do's" only six days later. It *was* the '60s, after all.

From the time I was a freewheelin' little cutie in pigtails, my father let me know that I had my *place*, which was in "the box." I was too fearful of evoking his militant wrath to ever seriously entertain the notion of crawling out of this box that was custom-made just for me. Common sense restricted my defiant nature, but my soul was never fooled; it was running around in panicked circles, pleading with me to speak out and bust loose from my emotional prison. For countless hours, I'd lie on my bed, fantasizing over words of dignity I'd love to have roll from my tongue in protest of everything my Air Force father and his black-and-white world stood for.

Of course, being so young and so obedient, these thoughts remained strictly fantasies. That is, until that chilly October day when my mother arrived home toting *Bob Dylan's Greatest Hits* under her arm. "I bought this for you, sweets." she said, which elicited a sneering, "Yeah, right." I figured anything she would be into couldn't possibly relate to me in even the remotest sense. "You're going to hear this. Got me?" she replied with an edge in her voice. In a half-hearted attempt to humor her and get her off my back, I took my place on the couch and rolled my eyes as she gingerly placed the needle on the vinyl.

Minutes into first hearing Bob's voice, I was certain my initial instincts about his music were right on target. Still, something about it stayed with me. Later that night, I crept out of bed to make a date with our den's stereo to hear those songs again...and again...and again. By the end of the week, I knew every word to every track on the record. Never before had anyone presented me with such freedom and vision. That magnificent strength and attitude woven throughout his lyrics gave me hope for an individuality I'd never thought possible in the confines of my tight little box. Finally, *finally*, I had found a voice to articulate my yearnings, my resentment, and my vulnerability.

Seven years later, in September 1990, the day arrived when I was graced with the opportunity to attend one of his shows. I remember the drive up to Birmingham, Alabama, with my best buddy, whom I had converted to Dylanism several months earlier. *Highway 61 Revisited* and assorted other Dylan masterpieces screamed out of the cassette player of his beat-up Sunbird. It was a magical evening, and I was Cinderella on my way to the ball. Hours later, I was perched out under the stars, the autumn breeze blowing across my face and sifting through my hair, listening as intently as a child to Bobby (with only his acoustic guitar) crooning the traditional lullaby, "Barbara Allen." His voice caressed each word like a graceful lover: "Young man, I think you're dying." I felt I, too, could die happily right then and there, as I savored every smirk and every nervous brush of those wild curls.

As the end of the show inevitably approached, and "Blowin' in the Wind" was winding down, I dashed to the edge of the stage and stared up at him in utter disbelief. During the last two or three minutes, I could have sworn he was looking directly at me. After commanding myself not to faint, I eyeballed him back. For all of 15 seconds, those piercing, bright-blue eyes bore directly into mine until I could take this pseudo-intimacy jive no longer. Like some sort of rough-and-ready Annie Oakley, I hiked up my long peasant skirt and began to climb up past the barriers to plant a kiss on that "childish mouth," as Joan Baez so beautifully described it. At that very moment, a brute of a security guard grabbed my hem, yanked me back down to reality, and growled, "Don't even *think* about it, sister."

Minutes later, Bobby Dylan strummed his last chord, flashed his last lightning-quick grin, softly spoke his last "Thanks ever'body," and was gone. ("The Vanishing American," as Bobby Neuwirth once quipped.) The overwhelming evening had drawn to a close. As other concert-goers filed out of the arena chatting, laughing, and arranging rides back home, I stood rooted in my grassy spot for what seemed like ages—hypnotized, speechless, and *aching*, really, for more of the conjurer's magic.

On the way home, my buddy and I didn't speak. No "Tombstone Blues" screaming out of the cassette player, no cheap conversational, "Wow, great show, huh?" Just a highway of diamonds with nobody on it, and a spiritual, sacred feeling swelling inside our souls we wanted to savor as long as possible. Later, when I mentioned this strange silence to him, he said, "I was too moved to speak. I was afraid if I did, it would have shattered the sounds inside my mind. Do you know what I mean?" Did I know what he meant? Was that some kind of joke?

Over the years of attending his concerts, I discovered I wasn't the only one who had fantasies of making some sort of connection with Bob Dylan. Standing in line at shows, nearly every fan I encountered shared memories of having met him or dreams of doing so. And with every single tale at every single venue, I was enthralled by these conversations. I wondered if others might be, too. Thus came the idea for this book.

Bob, you've given so many of us voices. So many of us have received courage and dignity through your words. You've touched the lives of the gentle, the inarticulate, the guardians, the protectors of the mind, the aching, the wounded, the luckless, the abandoned, and the forsaken. Now, it's time that we lifted up *our* voices to you, to give thanks for getting multitudes of us out of our boxes and into our own minds.

And very special thanks to all the people whose help and support made this book possible, starting with every Dylan fan around the world who took the time to submit their encounters for publication. We couldn't have done it without you, guys. Thanks also to my publisher, editor, and friend Jon Sievert, Chuck Gladden, Mike Corley, Marion Stevens, Maura Cain, Dale Minor, Richard Parker, Michael Ford (may you rest in peace), Renata Augenstein, Nicole Brennan, Mrs. Clara Hill, Joel Bernstein, Robert Goodman, Boston Woodard, Denis Telgemeier, Richard Leeds, Tom Mulhern, and Martha Arroyo-Neves. Most of all, thanks to my higher power for giving me the strength to believe again.

1956

Memories of a North Country Girl

Margaret Stark *attended high school with Bob Dylan and still lives in Hibbing, Minnesota. She retired from her secretarial job in 1989, when she was diagnosed with multiple sclerosis.*

I first met Bobby Zimmerman in 1956. He and my brother Joey used to pal around together in our hometown of Hibbing, Minnesota. Because we are of Italian descent, my mother cooked many pasta dishes. It was because of her that Bobby tasted his first Italian pasta, and he just loved it.

Joey and Bobby usually came in very late, when I was already in bed, so I never paid much attention to him when he came to our house. My mother always waited up for them, though, keeping that pasta he loved so much warming on the stove. My parents loved having young people around, and they absolutely adored Bobby. Mom was great friends with Beattie, Bob's mother; they'd worked together at Feldman's department store for years. Mom and Dad were very mellow people who didn't seem to mind that Joey rarely came in before midnight since he'd started hanging out with the Zimmerman kid.

I never really had too much to say to Bob until my brother got a new car. God, how I wanted to drive that car. So, when Joey asked me to be Bob's date and accompany him and his girlfriend on a Saturday night, we made a deal. I would be Bob's date, but *only* if I got to drive. He agreed. Unfortunately, all I remember about the date is sitting in the front seat with Bobby, wondering why he wouldn't say anything. He was quiet as a little mouse. Sadly, my brother was later killed in Vietnam in 1963.

The one thing that stirred Bobby up was music. My future husband, Gary, used to hang out in the Zimmerman's basement, playing the horn while Bobby plunked away on an old guitar for hours on end. Unfortunately, there were many people in Hibbing who mistreated Bob. Even back then, he had ideas about how "his music" should sound, and, quite frankly, people thought he was nuts. He'd sit on a little stool in the school auditorium with that harmonica around his neck and bang away on his guitar. The kids whispered, talked, and laughed, not even listening to him. They thought, "What in the world is this? We shouldn't have to hear this sort of junk. We should be listening to Elvis." Were *they* wrong.

When the Class of 1959 held its 10-year reunion at the Hibbing Moose Club, Gary and I were there. There'd been talk that Bob planned to attend, but no one knew for sure until my mother—who was there helping out—told us Bob was upstairs. He was too nervous to come down to the gathering, so we decided to go up and get him. We found him and his wife, Sara, sitting in the corner of an otherwise empty room. Bob introduced us to Sara, who was very pregnant, and told us he didn't want her in a big crowd of people, because of the baby. She was such a fragile little thing. We convinced them to accompany us downstairs, where we sat together in a secluded corner of the dimly lit Club.

In no time at all, people noticed he'd arrived and swarmed around. People who'd treated him like a joke in high school, and never had time for him, now wanted his autograph. Suddenly, they wanted to be his best friend. After an hour or so of this hypocrisy, he'd had enough and asked us for a ride to the airport. They left that night.

About five years ago, Hibbing High celebrated its 100-year anniversary with an enormous party. Again, former classmates speculated on the probability of Bob Dylan coming "home" to take part in the festivities. I just thought, "Why the hell do you care if he comes? You never spoke nicely of him before he became famous, so why should you care about him now?" I've even heard rumors that Bob has started to say he's from Duluth, Minnesota. If the rumors are true, we understand his reasons even though it's utter nonsense. He's probably still angry at the way Hibbing mistreated him. Gary and I have spoken about this at great length and just wish that he'd contact us. He knows we were friends; he was one of us.

The people who live in his old house told us they've seen him drive up in an old station wagon with his mastiff dog in the passenger seat and park in the driveway. After 20 to 30 minutes, he cranks the engine up and drives away. Years ago, he'd occasionally knock on the door and ask to take a look around that old house.

My mother used to carry a thick address book in her purse that included Bob's mother's phone number. I was always tempted to contact her and ask her how Bobby was doing, but never did. We know that times have changed. Bob Zimmerman has become "Bob Dylan," and he's now a famous personality. But Gary and I will always remember him as that shy young man who sat in the Hibbing High School auditorium playing his heart out. We'd love to sit and reminisce with him about the old days and share children and grandchildren stories with him. I'd even cook him up some pasta; now that would bring back some memories.

1961

Restless Farewell

Mimi Fariña is *the founder/director of Bread & Roses, a non-profit organ-ization that has brought free entertainment to institutionalized people in an around the San Francisco Bay Area for 25 years. She's also a talented musi-cian and actor whose sister happens to be Joan Baez.*

I met Bob Dylan one June night in 1961 at Gerde's Folk City in Greenwich Village. My parents and I were in New York because we were traveling to Paris the next day, where we were to live for two years. My sister Joan said I just *had* to come down to this club and see the Village to enjoy that new thing that was going on. So, I did. I can almost remember what I was wearing.

We got to the club, and my first impression of Dylan was of this lit-tle guy pacing around in the back. He sang that night, but the impor-tant part for me was that I was introduced to him and others by Joan. There was a wonderful spirit in the place—lots of writers, lots of hover-ing, lots of discussions about songwriting. There was a real vibe and a def-inite uniqueness about the atmosphere of creative writers gathered together communicating to one another about their writing. It's some-thing we all hope to see in our lifetime, but it just doesn't happen that often. I think it happened here in San Francisco with the Beat Generation. The Village was a wonderful scene to step into at age 16.

John Byrne Cooke

Dylan and Mimi Fariña, 1964.

The night I was introduced to Dylan, there was an after-show party. I don't know if Joanie was interested in Dylan at that point, or if she was just being protective of me. But when he asked me to go to the party, my big sister stepped in and said, "No, she can't. She can't stay up late, because she's traveling tomorrow." So, my party-going wasn't permitted, and Joan eventually hustled me back to wherever we were staying. The next day, my mother, father, and I got on a ship and sailed off to Paris, where I found and bought Dylan's first album. On the cover, he was just a little pudgy-faced person with a cap on. I loved it, particularly because I knew Eric Von Schmidt, the guy who wrote the liner notes. I felt a connection and became quite a fan of that album.

By the time I returned to the United States in 1963, Joanie was taking him on her tours. She would usually do the first half of the show and then introduce this new songwriter, Bob Dylan, who she thought was wonderful. They would do a set of mostly his songs together.

One of my strongest memories from that time was when they played a show somewhere in the south—Alabama, I think. I was in the audience with my husband, Richard. My very favorite song of Dylan's is "The Lonesome Death of Hattie Carroll," and I always wanted to hear him sing it. When we were visiting backstage during the show, however, I noticed that Joan's manager, Manny Greenhill, was pacing around looking extremely agitated.

Apparently, they had gotten word from either the Ku Klux Klan or some other group that they'd better not sing "Hattie Carroll" or someone would die. There was a worried discussion backstage about whether they should do it or not, but, of course, they *did* do the song. For me, it was very, very tense because I was terrified that something would happen. It didn't, but I loved how they followed through with the song. The words to that song are very typical of the fervor that carried Bob in the early days.

Richard and I spent a lot of time with Bob and Joan in those early days, but I haven't seen or spoken with him for many years now. I can't forget how he treated my sister when their relationship ended.

Jon Sievert

1961

Born in Time

Patricia Maher *is a writer and part-time publicist. She is recently retired from her position as Fine Arts Director and Public Relations Manager for the world-famous Stanley Hotel that abutts Rocky Mountain National Park in Estes Park, Colorado. She currently lives in a log home on her 37 acres in the Sangre de Christo mountains of southern Colorado.*

In 1961, Greenwich Village was a wonderful haven for artists, poets, writers, and musicians. I was a college drop-out, working for the *Village Voice* and waitressing part-time at the Cafe Figaro, when I first saw and heard Bob Dylan.

I was at a table in Gerde's Folk City with a gang of friends, and Bob sat in with Ramblin' Jack Elliott. When Dylan left the stage, we all looked at each other and I said, "He's better than anyone else who's played tonight." At that point, everyone started arguing whether they loved or hated him. I thought he was unbelievable. Others thought he was just this kid sitting in with well-known performers, and that he'd never go anywhere.

Everybody kind of knew everyone else. We all hung out at the same bar called the Kettle of Fish. We were all working in the arts—writing, acting, playing music, painting—and doing restaurant jobs, or whatever it took to get by, until we became famous. Dylan actually did it. I talked to him a few times, but he was usually very quiet when I was around him.

When I first saw him around the village, he was just doing solo guitar stuff. But within two years, he had a little entourage. His friend Bobby Neuwirth kept people away from him, as if he were already famous. He didn't want Bob talking to anyone. In a way, it's sad that happened, because there were many extraordinary people exchanging ideas in the Village at the time. Bob missed out on a lot of that, because he was so protected by this little coterie of people. At one point, though, my ex-husband showed him some of his poems, and Bob wrote him a little note.

The day his first album came out, someone brought it to the Cafe Figaro, and we played it over our sound system. The whole place fell silent. People were asking, "Who is that? He sounds so familiar." I said, "That's the kid that we see around all the time, Bob Dylan." The Cafe Figaro was a real hub, because it was at the corner of Bleecker and MacDougal Streets. I remember the day when Sara Lowndes came in and said, "Guess what, everyone? Bobby and I are engaged."

The first time I heard Dylan perform "Walls of Red Wing," I remember thinking, "My God, he's from Minnesota." At the time, he wasn't telling anyone that he was Robert Zimmerman from the Midwest; he had completely reinvented himself. But I had lived in Minnesota, and everyone there knew that if you were a bad kid, they sent you to the Red Wing reformatory in Minneapolis. Nobody I knew in New York had that specific point of reference.

After I left New York, I kind of kept in touch with Bob musically, but I never saw him again until Saturday, May 22, 1976, the night before the Rolling Thunder Revue played Fort Collins, Colorado. From Thursday, May 20 through Sunday, May 23, Dylan and his band stayed at the Stanley Hotel in Estes Park, about 35 miles west of Fort Collins.

Estes Park was a very conservative town, and while some of its citizens knew who Bob was, many didn't—or didn't care. It was a very small mountain community, which is why Dylan came up there to rehearse. in the first place. They knew there wouldn't be tons of fans hanging out. They'd have been swamped if they'd rehearsed in Fort Collins.

I wasn't working for the hotel at the time, but I *was* living in Estes Park. The night before the show, we all went up to the Stanley to listen to them rehearse in the concert room and music hall. We were able to watch them, because it was almost impossible to close off a public room in the Stanley. They were so loud, they literally *shook* the place.

I remember Bob was driving an Excalibur, a huge 1920s-style car that looked like something you'd see in the Great Gatsby. It was one of only 25 like it in the world. It had running boards, the works. I guess Bob was doing pretty well financially at the time.

Of course, we all went to the Rolling Thunder Revue. Tickets were $9.00, with a 25-cent parking charge. Seems unreal, now. The concert started at 1:00 P.M., and it *poured* rain for the next eight hours. After much dismay, we finally just gave up and let the rain roll down our faces. Hour after hour, you'd think, "This is insane. Go out to the van. This is crazy." But the fascination with Bob and his band was just incredible. There was no way in heck that you were going to leave.

That's the last time I saw him, but I still pay attention to him when he's in the news. He seems happier in the last few years, especially since he won the Grammy. All of a sudden, you're seeing pictures of him laughing. When he won the Grammy, he talked more than I ever heard him talk in my life. He appears to have turned his attitude around about some things, including his fans.

1961

Nothing was Delivered

Journalist **Nat Hentoff** *is a national treasure whose writing on music, journalistic responsibility, and First Amendment rights has set standards for excellence for half a century. A prolific author with more than a dozen books to his credit, he writes a regular column for the* Washington Post *and the* Village Voice. *He's best known to Bob Dylan fans as the man who conducted the hilarious, legendary 1966* Playboy *interview.*

My wife and I lived around the corner from Gerde's Folk City in 1961, and we'd often go in to hear the musicians. That's where we first saw and met Dylan. We were particularly intrigued by Bob because of the Woody Guthrie line he was pursuing.

Early on, I regularly wrote about him in the *Village Voice* and profiled him for *New Yorker*, so *Playboy* called me to do that interview. At the time, I'd done a number of *Playboy* interviews, and the rule then was that the interviewee had to see the transcript before it was published. Looking back, I don't know why that was ever allowed to happen. Anyway, I did a straightforward interview with him at Columbia studios that went quite well. But when he got the edited transcript back from the magazine, he was furious because they'd screwed it up and put words in his mouth.

When he called me one Saturday morning to complain, I told him, "Just tell them to go to hell. After all, Bob, they need your permission." He said, "No, we're going to do another one, and we're going to do it right now." I just had a pen and paper; I didn't have my tape recorder with me right then. My arm almost fell off trying to keep up. During the interview, I played the straight man. He was improvising stream-of-consciousness stuff right there on the spot. Some of it was incredibly funny. Every time I'd feed him some dumb question—because I knew what the game was—he somehow managed to run with it.

In the early part of his career, he was always interested in articles written about him. But after he got famous, he became pretty much removed, though we actually lived in the same neighborhood awhile. That was okay with me. Right before the Rolling Thunder Revue tour, my wife wrote a piece about Dylan in the *New York Times* Arts & Leisure section, in which she said something along the lines of, "Bob's not a kid anymore. Some of the freshness is gone." Right around the same time, I got my only assignment from *Rolling Stone*, a story detailing the Rolling Thunder tour. I made some inquiries through his management and asked to speak with him. They told me that Bob was very angry over my wife's article, and that he refused to speak with me. Apparently, It was guilt by association.

So, I said, "The hell with him." I had friends on the tour, including Joan Baez, Allen Ginsburg, and several of the guys in Bob's band. So I interviewed them all and was just about to send the piece to *Rolling Stone* when some emissary of Dylan's phoned me up and said, "Mr. Dylan will now speak to you." With great pleasure I said, "It's too late...I don't need him."

1962

Long Ago, Far Away

Marc Silber, *aka Big Boy Once, is a musician, luthier, and vintage instrument dealer who lives in Berkeley, California. In 1963, he opened Fretted Instruments in Greenwich Village, which quickly became the gathering point for the musicians who helped shape the folk revival of that era. A typical day might find Mississippi John Hurt, Elizabeth Cotten, John Sebastian, Maria Muldaur, David Grisman, and Mance Lipscomb hanging out and jamming. He is currently the owner of Marc Silber Music in Berkeley and can be reached through his web site at* www.marcsilbermusic.com.

In 1961, I was a student at the University of Michigan, more interested in learning to play guitar than studying English, history, or economics. The great folk and blues revival was really starting to grow, and we had a small group of people who got together regularly to listen to music, talk about it, and learn how to play it.

A few of the players were quite advanced, and the rest of us were learning from them. One of the good ones was from New York, so a few of us decided we'd go there on sort of a field trip over one of the school holidays. The first folk place we went to was the Gaslight on MacDougal Street, where there was a hootenanny going on. For those too young to remember, a hootenanny was a show where a lot of people each did three or

24

four songs. I remember it well because Reverend Gary Davis was there, and his singing and guitar playing just blew my mind. Then Dylan came on with Jim Kweskin, and they did ragtime songs with the kazoo—just razzmatazz sort of stuff. I thought they were terrific. What really thrilled me, though, was that they were my age and doing this old stuff.

The next time I really thought about him was when our little group was helping plan the 1962 University of Michigan Folk Festival, as it was called then. It wasn't the grand size that it later became as the Ann Arbor Folk Festival, but they were starting to have concerts with audiences of about 3,000 people. We had this ongoing discussion about why folk songs had to be old. How come you couldn't write a folk song? It was always a big topic. We decided that since Woody Guthrie did it, it was possible to write a folk song, but we didn't know how to do it.

Then I remembered that Dylan was doing the same sort of thing—creating songs that you thought were old. So, I said, "Why don't we just get Bob Dylan in the concert?" His album hadn't come out yet, so only those of us who'd gone to New York knew who he was. But we convinced them to put him on the show. Somebody drove Dylan from New York City and back, and we paid him a grand total of something like $100 for the weekend, including the car and driver. He did a few songs on Saturday and performed an entire concert by himself on Sunday.

That was a really good festival with a lot of terrific people like Jesse Fuller, Danny Kalb, Jim Kweskin, and Nick Gravenites. I was asked to participate, even though I'd only been playing a year or so and didn't sing too much. I think I was really confident with about three songs, but one of them was Dylan's "Song to Woody." The first album came out a month or so before the festival, so I had a chance to learn it. Of course, it made me feel hip to do a Dylan song. Just about everyone in the audience was hearing him for the first time, and I already knew one of his songs. While I was warming up backstage, he poked his head in, and I said, "Hey, Bob, I just want to tell you I'm going to sing a song off your album. I hope you don't mind." He sort of growled, "rruuuuuhhh." I told him, "Well, it's too late now because I only know three songs, and that's one of them," and he laughed.

Dylan didn't seem to want to hang with us; he really wasn't the friendliest type of fellow in those situations. But I think about it now and realize he was thinking about a very different world than we were. It was way

U of M

FOLK FESTIVAL

APRIL 20,21,22

FRIDAY   8 p.m.
JESSE FULLER
union ballroom 90¢

SATURDAY 10:30 a.m.
WORKSHOP
both FREE   S.A.B.
LECTURE   2 p.m.

HOOTENANNY
TRUEBLOOD AUD.
8:30 pm $1.50, $2

SUNDAY   2 p.m.
BOB DILLON
union ballroom 90¢

PERRY LEDERMAN
DANNY KALB
PAUL PRESTOPINO
MIKE SHERKER
JOEL MYERSON
MARC SILBER
JESSE FULLER
BOB DILLON
   and many others

from

OBERLIN, M.S.U,
CHICAGO, W.S.U,
WISC., CAL., N.Y.

Poster for the 1962 University of Michigan Folk Festival. You could have seen Bob *Dillon* for only 90¢ at the Sunday matinee. Note author's name on the program at right.

advanced. He was already an artist; we were just thinking we'd become artists, because it was more fun than being a worker. Dylan had a much more purposeful musical existence; he had something to do.

There was also a curious personal side note to that festival. My sister's school roommate was the daughter of Walter Reuther, the president of the United Autoworkers Union and one of the most powerful men in the country. He and his brother Victor had been severely beaten, shot at, and had acid thrown on them while walking the picket lines in the '30s, when the autoworkers were trying to unionize. They'd actually fought and put their lives on the line for freedoms we now enjoy. We figured Walter would love this guy who was so much like Woody Guthrie, so we convinced him to come to the Sunday concert. But to our surprise, he was infuriated by Dylan's arrogance and didn't much like him at all. We loved him. Bob was a master at figuring out the hook and recrafting old songs to make them his.

By fall of 1963, I'd moved to New York and was living in the Village. I'd originally gone just to hang out awhile, and had brought several really nice vintage instruments with me. When I was ready to leave, I tried selling one to finance my trip. Much to my surprise, no one wanted to pay anything for them or actually knew much about them. So I was complaining to Izzy Young, who ran the New York Folklore Center. He said, "Well, I don't know anything about them. When people ask me to sell something on consignment, I just ask how much? I don't ask if it's fair."

He'd had quite a few good instruments over the years and said he thought it would be a good idea if someone opened up a guitar shop. Then he said, "Hey, I just saw a guy put a sign in a window this morning around the corner. Let's go look at it." So off we went, and suddenly I was in business. I started Fretted Instruments with exactly four bucks in my pocket. We opened in late November, the week after President Kennedy was assassinated. The minute I opened for business, the first customers in the door were Dylan and Joan Baez. He bought some fingerpicks for a quarter.

He was around the Village a lot during that time, and was friends with people I knew, mainly Artie and Happy Traum. I opened at noon, so Artie sometimes taught guitar in the back of the store in the morning. At one point, Dylan, or maybe it was Artie, suggested we get together on Saturday mornings to swap songs before the students showed up. The third time we met, I got there early to open the door and there were about 30-35 kids milling around. There was a movie theater on the ground floor below my shop, so I was thinking maybe they were waiting to get in there. But it was 8:00 in the morning, so I asked them, "What's going on?" They said, "We hear Bob Dylan hangs out in one of these stores on Saturdays." I said, "What?" but was thinking, "Oh, noooo." We managed to get together that day, but the next week there were about 200 kids milling around. We knew then it was over. If Dylan had showed up that day, he wouldn't have even been able to get inside the shop. By then, his second record was out, the one with "Blowin' in the Wind," and he was starting to become very important to a lot of people.

Soon he couldn't even go out, and that had a profound effect on me. He was the first person I knew who got so famous that he couldn't even go out tripping around being nobody. Once you're somebody like that, you can't just be nobody. Dylan was highly energetic in those early years. The liner notes on the back of his record albums had a certain kind of flow to them, with him writing about the lyrics and the dreams about the lyrics. I think he was highly motivated by magic substances.

I didn't really see him too much after that, although I sold him a couple of guitars along the way during the '60s. That 1930s Gibson Nick Lucas

Special he played in "Don't Look Back" had belonged to my sister. It was in mint condition when I sold it to him, but it got a little wrecked. He had that guitar for a long time. Later, probably in the early '70s, I drove up to Woodstock to sell him a really nice late-'60s Martin. He was a tough guy to do business with, though, because he didn't have any idea what the guitars were worth.

That's the last time I talked to him. But I do remember coming back from Tangier with my girlfriend in 1975 and hearing that song with the line, "She might be in Tangier" ["If You See Her, Say Hello"]. I always wanted to ask him, "Hey, Bob, what's *that* about?" The last time I saw him play was in 1987, and I thought he was fabulous. It was with the Grateful Dead at the Oakland Coliseum. The sound was perfect, and the Dead blended well with Dylan.

The real Dylan I knew was in *Don't Look Back*. It really shows how candid he was and how playful and creative he could be while dealing with stardom. He's a great artist. I especially like his piano playing. And he's a great singer to be able throw a rhythm on an old song to get it in the mood he's in that day. I really like that.

The Times
They Are A Changin'

Michael Perlin, *53, is a professor at New York Law School, specializing in all aspects of mental disability law. He is married with two children (ages 15 and 17, both veteran Dylan concert-goers) and plays clarinet in a community concert band.*

Two of my most indelible memories are linked to the civil rights march on August 8, 1963. The first occurred several months before at Gerde's Folk City, where I'd gone to see a relatively unknown folksinger named Bob Dylan. After listening intently to his first set, I dropped a quarter into his fedora hat. He expressed his appreciation with a self-conscious, boyish grin and a half-whispered, "Thanks, man."

On the day of the march, I was 17 and had just finished my freshman year in college. I was working on Capitol Hill for Congressman Edward J. Patten (D-NJ), a strong supporter of civil rights. Congressman Patten had been given a VIP ticket for the march, but, because of prior commitments, he passed it on to me. As I took my assigned seat, I found myself positioned between actor James Garner and the pop/gospel singer, Brook

Benton. Benton was wearing alligator shoes, which I'd never seen before in my young life. Both of them asked me repeatedly if I realized the enormity of what was happening. Benton said, "Son, this is a turning point in American history. You'll understand it when you get a bit older."

By then, Dylan had exploded into the public's consciousness and had been invited (along with Joan Baez, Peter, Paul & Mary, Odetta, and others) to sing at that historic event. And sing he did, as "Blowin' in the Wind" and "Only A Pawn in Their Game" rang out across the masses. It was at that moment that popular music, culture, and politics became fused forever into the American soul.

> *"I remember being moved by Bob Dylan's song, "Blowin' in the Wind," which I had the pleasure of hearing him perform during the civil rights march on Washington in 1963. The song so beautifully captured the longing for a more humane and peaceful world. Mr. Dylan, whom I met briefly in 1970 when we both received honorary degrees from Princeton, also wrote a number of ballads that showed great compassion for the struggles of black people. By any measure, he has had a profound impact on the growth of popular music."*
>
> *—Coretta Scott King*

Changing of the Guards

Rowland Scherman *served as the first photographer for the Peace Corps in 1961, and his work has been displayed on the covers and in the pages of* Life, Time, Newsweek, Paris Match, Playboy, *and* National Geographic. *In 1968, he won a Grammy for the cover of* Bob Dylan's Greatest Hits, *and published a photo book called* Elvis is Everywhere *in 1991. Now 60, he lives in Birmingham, Alabama. His first encounter with Dylan was at the 1963 Newport Folk Festival.*

Peter, Paul & Mary were huge, the Kingston Trio were huge, and both groups were going to be at the Newport Folk Festival. Then, in passing, little Bobby Dylan showed up to sing with Joan Baez and turned things around like Clay over Liston. That weekend looms as the turning point in his career. He came in there driving an old Ford truck, wearing a bullwhip around his neck, and sporting a wry, quizzical look; he left as the new king. He had the goods, but nobody really knew who the hell he was. And because he wasn't that attractive, no one was crowding around him, either.

Newport, 1963. *Photos: Rowland Scherman*

I was mildly familiar with his work at the time, and he was so approachable. There I was, standing a foot in front of him with a 35mm lens, and I said, "I'd like to do a story about you." He said, "That'd be fine, that'd be cool." He wasn't guarded or anything like that. He wanted it. In those days not many people wanted to do a story about him, so when I suggested it, he was all for it. Too bad I didn't follow up on it. I

had no idea what sort of story I'd do; I just knew he was coming along, and that he was cool.

He shook up the world of folk music that weekend. On Friday, he did a duet with Joanie. The next night, Peter, Paul & Mary sang a couple of his songs, and Joanie also invited him up for her set. By the end of the weekend, he was centerstage. Peter, Paul & Mary were behind him, Pete Seeger was behind him, and Theodore Bikel was way behind him.

The next time I saw him was 1967, when I was married, living in D.C., and shooting pictures for *Life* every day. Dylan did a concert at the Washington Coliseum, which was about a six-iron shot right up the street from where I lived. So, me and the wife decided to check it out. I brought a Nikon with a 300mm lens and a couple rolls of film.

After a few tunes, I said to my wife, "This is great. I'm going to take a few shots. I'll be right back." I went to the backstage door and was told no one was allowed backstage. I just said, "*Life* magazine, out of my way, fuck you." I just wouldn't be denied; I was in the zone. I'd just shot a *Life* cover, and there were pictures of mine in the magazine every week. Whatever my aura was, it was enough to bullshit my way backstage; it didn't take that much. Dylan was in that dirty blue spot, doing some song I can no longer remember. I put the 300 mill on him, and I could see the whole thing. His hair, his halo, his harp—the three H's.

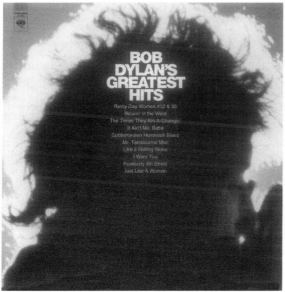

So, I went bang, bang, bang, bang—six or seven frames. No motor or anything. Then, I said, "Thank you very much, I'll be leaving now." I didn't hang around. I just kept thinking, "It doesn't get any better than this," and went back to watch the rest of the concert.

When I got the pictures back, I went up to New York and showed them to John Byrd, the art director at Columbia Records. He'd been dating my sister at the time. John flipped through the pictures and said, "That's the next cover." Everything should be that easy. It actually happened faster than the process of retelling it. A few months later, the cover was out.

I remember Byrd asking me, "Is $300 fine for you?" I said, "Yeah, that's *great*. Thanks a lot, John." I got the check, cashed it, the album comes out, and that's it. The darned thing is still in production. It was actually supposed to be the cover for *Blonde on Blonde*, but Dylan told his people, "No, I don't want that to be the cover," so it wasn't. But his contract lapsed right when they were about to do the *Greatest Hits* album, so Byrd snuck it in there when Bob didn't have the power to stop it.

Four or five months after the album comes out, Byrd calls and says, "Rowland, we're up for a Grammy. Do you want to come to New York?" I said, "That's great," but the weather was lousy—huge snowstorm—and I declined. He said, "Aw, don't worry about it. We don't have a chance anyway." The next day I got a telegram saying, "Congratulations, you're now the Grammy-award-winning...blah, blah, blah." Who knows? Maybe if I'd made the trip, we might have lost.

The Grammy shows up, and my name's misspelled, just like it is on the album. Not only that, but the gramophone part was broken. I packed it back up and said, "Thanks a lot, but spell my name right and send me another Grammy." *Never* heard from them again. What knocks me out now is that he's turned out to be one of the icons of the '60s. That makes me proud, along with the fact that it's in the Library of Congress. I later asked a lawyer to check into unlawful enrichment. I mean, they sold 40 million albums, and I got 300 bucks. I think maybe they should give me a gold star or $20,000.

A couple of years later, when *Bob Dylan's Greatest Hits, Volume II* came out, Mary Travers' husband duplicated my picture for the cover. It was almost the same thing, only not quite as dark or graphic, and Dylan okayed that cover for some reason. Byrd said, "Bob, you little bastard. You didn't want the other one, which was the same thing." Bob just sort of tucked his head under his arm and was all sheepish about it. I guess he realized he was wrong.

Never Gonna
Be the Same Again

Bill Amatneek *was the bassist on the first David Grisman Quintet album, and he has recorded with Mark O'Connor, Kate Wolf, Darol Anger, and the Chambers Brothers. His stories about music life have appeared in* Rolling Stone, Down Beat, *and* Bluegrass Unlimited, *and he's told them at bluegrass, folk, and storytelling festivals. His book,* Acoustic Stories, *will be published in March, 2000, by Vineyards Press. Bill can be reached through his web site,* www.Amatneek.com.

Back in 1963, I was a banjo pickin', string-bass slappin', Philadelphia folkie. Because Philly is only a two-hour drive from New York, what went down in the Big Apple was soon known in the City of Brotherly Love, and it didn't take long for us to hear about Bob Dylan.

The folk scene was small then, and broken into camps. There were bluegrass boys, blues people, old-timey folks, ragtime fans, traditional balladeers, political singers, and the Internationalists.

But Dylan, it was said, belonged to none of these; he was into something else. Well, sure, *some* of his songs were political, but not all. And the ones that *were* political were not in-your-face, "We-Shall-Not-Be-

Moved" types. They were subtler, more symbolic, like "Blowin' in the Wind." Because of folks talking and the reporting of *Sing Out!* magazine, everyone, in every corner of the Philly folk scene, was well aware of Bob Dylan and looking forward to his first local gig.

So the evening finally arrives, May 3, 1963, shortly before his second album comes out. It's at the Ethical Culture Society Hall, in downtown Philadelphia. The seating is 300 souls exactly—that's what the sign over the front door says—and Bob has the hall filled.

But showtime comes and showtime goes, and Dylan has not stepped onstage. Because I arrived early, I have a front row seat. Seeing a door 10 feet in front of me that leads backstage, I decide to go looking for him. I step through the door and see a hallway leading to the wings, steps going up to the catwalk, and still more steps leading down. I go down, and after some staircase twists and blind corridors, I spot Dylan. He's alone: no manager, no agent, and no entourage. Just him, his guitar, and a harmonica. At the moment I set eyes on him, he's backing out of a janitor's closet, having wisely decided that it is not the way to the stage. He looks vibrant, bright-eyed, inner-driven, inner-held, and lost.

I say, "Lookin' for the stage, Bob?"

"Yeah."

"This way." I lead him up to stage level and point him to the wings.

"Thanks, man," he says.

There were two sets that evening, with a good break in between, so we all went outside. The feeling was unanimous: no matter which folk camp you came from, you recognized Dylan's genius and saw he was doing something that had not been done before. No one who wrote songs was also performing them. Okay, *some* folks, such as Pete Seeger, were writing *some* of their own material, but almost everything Dylan did was his own work, and it was deeply personal. His lyrics didn't necessarily expose who Dylan was, but they exposed how he felt, which was urgently and fervently.

And certainly no one sang like Dylan. He shouted his vocals and harangued you with his nasalized, ear-searing twang. His midwesternese, now copied by so many singers, was entirely new. Sometimes, he'd squeeze more words into a line than its meter could handle and still get away with it poetically

There were some who said he could not sing at all. Dylan broke the rules of singing. He'd take a breath in the middle of a word, fergoshsakes, and even folkies knew you didn't do that. His absorption in each song was mesmerizing and consistently put you into the Dylan haze. There were no introductions, no small talk. He didn't try to charm, entertain, or even perform for us. He simply dove into the song, executed it, and tore it asunder.

A harmonica? *No one* was putting a harmonica on a holder and playing along with guitar. Most harpists back then played cross harp, sucking in on the notes to bend and bluesify them. But Dylan mostly played straight harp; he blew out to play, and the melodies he blew were his own jingle-jangle.

Sure, there were some folks who complained that he was a strummer, not a picker, but his strumming was relentless; it drove his song into you. With his bouncing harmonica, pushed vocals, and hypnotic guitar accompaniment, he was a three-piece, one-man band. It was clear he had questioned some major cornerstones of folk music, from creation through performance, and come back with new answers. Dylan was riveting.

I remember seeing *The Freewheelin' Bob Dylan* in the window of a record shop a couple of weeks later and thinking that a sea change was taking place. A new era of the songwriter-as-performer was beginning. After Dylan, whether you were folk, rock, R&B, bluegrass, or country, when you went onstage, you sang your own song.

Yeah, I know what you're thinking: "Bill, if you hadn't gone back there, dredged Dylan up from the depths of that auditorium and got him on stage that evening, why, Bob Dylan might never have made it. He might have missed his first Philly gig, blown his reputation, killed his career then and there, and never gone on to...lead the revolution."

Well, that's mighty kind of you, but somehow I just don't think so.

1965

Pledging My Time

Mel Prussack *is, by his own reckoning, arguably Bob Dylan's greatest fan. When you examine the evidence, he makes a good case. The 58-year-old pharmacist from Old Bridge, New Jersey, has been a fan for 35 years and maintains a Dylan shrine and museum in his home that's open to the public by appointment. He can be contacted at* melp@voicenet.com.

On February 17, 1965, while lying in bed flipping through the channels on my television set, I saw and heard Bob Dylan singing "It's Alright Ma (I'm Only Bleeding)" on the Les Crane Show. Though I only heard part of the song, it changed my life forever. I immediately ran out to get the record, only to find that the album it was on, *Bringing It All Back Home*, was not out yet. So, I bought all his other records and discovered all those other great songs. I was completely hooked, and I've been collecting everything related to him since.

I really started my whole Dylan kick by filming him. In the early days, before cameras were banned in concert halls, and before video, I captured portions of his concerts on Super-8 film. My amateur film footage was the first of what has now become a major industry.

40

Now, I have stuff all over the house. When my daughter got married, I took over her room and then outgrew that. Eventually, the collection turned into a little museum that I call The Dylan Shrine. It's in a 12' by 20' room in my home, and there's not an empty spot in it. I keep changing the exhibits and constantly adding new things, just because there is so much. The criteria for inclusion is that it has to be about Dylan or Dylan-related. For instance, I also have exhibits on the Traveling Wilburys and the Wallflowers, his son Jakob's band.

Mel Prussack in The Dylan Shrine.

There are literally thousands of items in the Shrine, including some 700 vinyl albums. On just Dylan alone, I've got about 500 bootlegs from around the world and another 400 Dylan-related CDs that include either Dylan or one of his songs. My Dylan library has almost every book ever written about him, and there are about 200. One of my prized possessions is a signed copy of the *Don't Look Back* book in paperback, along with a photo of D.A. Pennebaker signing it.

I also collect Dylan fanzines from around the world; a new one just came out in Poland. I've got them all, including every *Telegraph* and every *Isis* from issue number one and all the early ones going back to the '60s, like *Look Back* and *Talkin' Bob Zimmerman Blues*. In the '60s, '70s, and '80s, there were beautiful Dylan fanzines coming out of England, Germany, and Italy, but the United States had nothing, really, until *On the Tracks*. It took too many years for it to come along. Bob is an artist who still does not get enough credit in his own country for his cultural contributions.

"Mr. Tambourine Man" Zim-Art hat.

Other items include a Dylan set list and several of his guitar picks. I've also got a few gold record awards; the one that means the most to me is *Highway 61 Revisited*. Bob has also been on seven postage stamps around the world, and I have all of them.

Some of the most interesting exhibits are examples of what I call "Zim-Art," objects that are created to represent either the title of a Dylan song, a line from one, or a Dylan album title. Bob Dylan took an old discarded tune called "No More Auction Block" and turned it into "Blowin' in the Wind." I do the same thing with Zim-Art. My most famous piece of Zim-Art is called "Mr. Tambourine Man," which is constructed on a hat that I wear to every Dylan concert. I've also created 80 or 90 Dylan clocks that I call "Dyl-Time." They're all individually marked with a Dylan quote relating to time.

Now, I'm getting people to create and send in their own Zim-Art. Fans from all over the world participate in a contest I run on the "Expecting Rain" web site [*www.execpc.com/~billp61/boblink.html*]. We've got a "Mystery Zim-Art" contest going on right now. Once a month, I put the entries on the web site, and fans from all over the world respond. I send a Dylan postcard to the first person who e-mails the name of the song that the piece of Zim-Art represents. It's been a lot of fun. I've done four or five contests already, and fans are always telling me how much they love it.

I also make silver Dylan key chains, each with a different picture of Bob on them. At a concert last year, I attached my card to one and tossed it up on the stage. At the end of the show, Dylan picked it up, read it, and then threw it back into the crowd of about 5,000 people. I knew the guy that caught it and told him that, because Bob had touched it, it had to go in the Shrine. Fortunately, he agreed. He didn't want to give it up, but he did, and I made a display of it. Around the display, I put all of the internet correspondence from people asking what Bob had thrown into the audience. Someone I knew from Long Island wrote a story explaining what it was.

I've taken my hobby and elevated it to the highest possible degree. I meet many Dylan fans at shows who are interested in visiting the Shrine. I screen them out a bit, and if they seem okay, I invite them over. I've had three students who've come to the Shrine to interview me and gather information for their thesis. Each got an *A* on their report.

The Shrine has given me a lot of visibility in the Dylan community. I took my son-in-law to the last Dylan concert I attended, and he told me I was like a celebrity because people kept coming over to talk to me. They know me because I wear the Zim-Art hat. I've also appeared in

Some of Prussack's Zim-Art "Dyl-Time" clocks.

two films with Bob. The first was *The 30th Anniversary Tribute Concert* in 1992. There's footage of me walking into the Garden wearing a *Slow Train Coming* tour jacket. The guy who was filming in the lobby asked me to walk through the doors and not turn around, but I wasn't going to miss out on the opportunity of being seen if the footage made it into the movie. I turned around and looked into the camera, and it ended up on the concert video and the laser disc.

The second film, which represents my greatest Dylan achievement

thus far, is shown at the Rock and Roll Hall of Fame. It's in an exhibit called "You Really Got a Hold on Me," which features fans of rock-and-roll personalities. In this particular clip, I am shown in The Dylan Shrine explaining Zim-Art. Later they redid it and added Dylan to the film. I talk about my "Mr. Tambourine Man" piece, and then it cuts to Bob singing the song. Then it cuts back to me. That made me think that Dylan or Dylan's people saw this film and allowed his footage to be put in with mine. I think he saw it, liked what he saw, and said, "Okay, I'll be in it with him."

The first time I saw Bob perform live was at the Concert for Bangladesh on August 1, 1971, at Madison Square Garden. Since then, I have never missed a Dylan tour within a 100-mile radius of my home; I catch one or two shows each time. I've traveled to Syracuse, New York, and Philadelphia, but because I've got a business, I can't get away as often as I'd like. The furthest I've traveled to see him was Cleveland, when they opened the Rock and Roll Hall of Fame. I knew he would show up for that, and I had to go to see my movie. Our local newspaper ran a picture of me wearing my Zim-Art hat with the headline, "Local Dylan Fan Earns Immortality at Rock Hall of Fame." The caption called me the "Dylanesque Druggist." After that, people who read the article came into my drug store (Bay Drugs) and asked to see some of my things. I've met so many great people that way. When you meet fellow Dylan fans, you discover a real bond.

I was also written up in the local paper when I won the Bob Dylan Imitators Contest at a Greenwich Village club called Speakeasy. I actually won it twice, despite the fact that I didn't imitate him at all. Instead, I performed parodies I wrote of Dylan songs. The judges included Larry "Ratso" Sloman (former Dylan biographer), Mike Porco (former owner of Gerde's Folk City), and Bob Fass (the long-time NYC radio personality). The parodies were later published in *Look Back* and in the 50th issue of the British fanzine *ISIS*.

When *The Bootleg Series* album came out, I wrote another parody called "Series of Schemes," which talks about the many different ways I've attempted to meet Dylan throughout the years. I'd planned to perform it at the Dylan Imitators Contest that year, but the Speakeasy club was sold and changed to a disco format. I'd made a video of it, though, and I really wanted Bob to see it. So, I sent it to his manager and asked for permission to enter it in a contest. Because I took Bob's voice out of the recording of "Series of Dreams" and replaced it with my voice reading my lyrics over the original music, I can't use it without permission.

Dylan knows who I am, though. I wear my "Mr. Tambourine Man" Zim-Art hat to all his concerts, and any time I've been close enough to the stage, he tips his hat. When he sees me, he gives me a look like, "Oh, I see *you're* here again." He definitely gives me some kind of acknowledgment. I've been told that he refers to me as "the nut from New Jersey," which I feel is a big compliment. I've never had the chance to meet him, but I've certainly tried. I've gone to his bus and tried to get in there, and I've hung out around his house, but it's very difficult. I'm still hoping I'll get to meet him someday.

The closest I've come was last year in Atlantic City. He was doing his final song, "Not Fade Away," when he saw a couple of girls dancing in the side aisle and signaled for them to come up onstage. Once those two girls got up there, a bunch of other girls also started jumping onstage. I was sitting right in front of the stage, and my wife told me I should go up there, too. I said, "No, it's all girls up there," and she said, "So?" I said, "Yeah, you're right," and climbed up on the stage wearing my Zim-Art hat. I walked right over to him, patted him on the back, and said, "Bob, you know we all love you." I patted him very gently because I know he's got a bad back, and I didn't want to hurt him. He had all these girls kissing and hugging him, so he didn't really respond to me. As I walked off the stage, I felt like Moses must have felt when he came down the mountain with the Ten Commandments. I was glowing, and it took me a few days to come down.

I'd made a special gift for him, but when I finally got close to him, I didn't have it with me. I didn't expect to walk up onstage that day. It's a toy called Tricky Dog, which is a black-and-white Scotty dog mounted on a magnet. It was a very popular and inexpensive toy in the '50s, and everybody had one. I'm sure Dylan did, too, so I went searching for one on eBay to give him. I found a couple and wrote a letter to go with them that says, "The Dylan Shrine of New Jersey would like Bob Dylan to accept this gift as a small token of thanks for his past and future endeavors as a song-and-dance man." I also included quotes from him that express why I think he'd enjoy the gift. In the past, he's said, "I'm rooted back in the '50s" and "There's a magnetic attraction where I was brought up." And any true Dylan fan knows how he feels about dogs. Years ago, he always toured with his dogs, but I don't know if he still does anymore. I signed the letter and mounted the Tricky Dogs to it. My plan is to get up close and show it to him. I know that when he sees it, his eyes will light up and he'll say, "Wow, I haven't seen one of those for 40 years." When I give him something like that he loves, I know he'll send me something back, like an autographed picture or something.

I'm still constantly adding to my Dylan collection, and it's so much easier today with the internet. I used to have to go to record shows all over the place to find things. Now, I can find almost anything online, because it's the whole world you're dealing with. It's a great thing. My quest will go on as long as Bobby Dylan continues to document our times. May it long continue for the enlightenment and ecstasy of those of us who "get it."

1965

Clean-Cut Kid

Michelle McFee *is a former publicist for the David Nelson Band and now works for record distributor City Hall Records in San Rafael, California. She was a 15-year-old high school student when she had her encounter with Bob, and tens of thousands witnessed it. On December 3, 1965, Dylan held a San Francisco press conference that was televised on KQED, the local PBS station. For nearly an hour, Dylan handled a roomful of largely clueless media people with an masterful blend of sincerity, put-on, annoyance, humor, and patience. Michelle's moment came near the end:*

MM: *Do you prefer songs with a subtle or obvious message?*
BD: *Uh, I don't really prefer those kinds of songs at all. Message? You mean like...? What song with a message?*
MM: *Well, like "Eve of Destruction," and things like that.*
BD: *Do I prefer that to what?*
MM: *I don't know, but your songs are supposed to have a subtle message.*
BD: *Subtle message? (chuckling). Where'd ya hear that?*
MM: *In a movie magazine.*
BD: *Oh, my God (lighting a cigarette and smiling). We don't discuss those things here.*

A round the time Dylan's first couple of albums came out, I had a friend whose older brother was into Bob, so we used to go over to her house and play the records all the time. I liked literature and language, so his songwriting really intrigued me. It was so different...so poetic. He started that whole evolution in the music business where listening to the lyrics became important.

People would say, "Oh God, that guy can't sing," and I'd say, "That's not what this is about. You don't *get* it. It's not about singing. If you want singing, go listen to Sinatra or something." There were so many people that just didn't understand. It seemed like people either really loved him or hated him. There wasn't much middle ground.

Sometime around October, I wrote a letter to Albert Grossman [Dylan's manager], asking if I could meet and interview Bob for my school newspaper when he came to town. When the press conference was set up, his office contacted my school and invited me to attend.

I was just trying to find out some things about his songs and had written a list of questions. Unfortunately, the only one I had the nerve to ask evoked the wrong response. I was a huge Bob Dylan fan and was mortified by his answer. Looking at the video many years later, I can see that he actually responded pretty gently to me. I didn't realize it at the time, because I was teased mercilessly at school after it happened. You know how teenagers are. They all said, "How could you have said that to Bob Dylan? How could you have quoted a movie magazine?" Well, I didn't know. That was my whole frame of reference at the time. I wrote a synopsis of the press conference for my high school newspaper, but didn't delve into anything personal. That would have ended up in the trash anyway, so I didn't even bother. And every time I managed to live down the experience, they'd show the press conference again on television.

I was embarrassed about the whole thing until I met Jerry Garcia about five years later. He thought the whole thing was a hoot and told me he was impressed as hell to meet *that* person. He and David Nelson had watched it together and spent the whole time cracking up at the pretentious questions being asked by the media.

Later on, people started telling me they had a video of the press conference. They all said, "Hey, were you that person?" "Yep, that was me." Back in the late '70s, I heard there was a place in the East Bay selling them, but I couldn't find the store and gave up looking for a copy. Eventually, somebody through the Grateful Dead tape traders network gave me one. By then, I could look at it in a different light. Dylan was really putting on a lot of those journalists at the press conference and was actually pretty nice to me.

All in all, it was a very brief encounter. After the interview, I went up and met Dylan and shook his hand. He was very nice, but there were people steering him away, so we didn't get the chance to stand and chat. I snatched the cigarette right out of his hand and took it home for a souvenir. I came across it a while ago; it was a Marlboro. After the press conference ended, I remember walking to the car with Allen Ginsberg and some woman. At the time, I didn't have a clue who Ginsberg was. Of course, after I found out, I ran over to the bookstore in Sausalito and bought a copy of *Howl*.

1969

Seeing the Real You at Last

Sam Field *"grew up in the 'sexties,' a few years younger than Bob. Although I always dug his sound, it wasn't until I got really high that I found out what he was actually saying, which is still a big secret to maybe 99% of his fans."*

June 1969: Dylan had been lying low since his motorcycle accident. Now he was scheduled to make a rare public appearance on *The Johnny Cash Show*, and his guest appearance was no minor event to those of us who loved his music.

I was hanging around a friend's apartment with several other kids, just wasting time. There was no television in the place, and I just had to watch Bob Dylan that night. Five minutes before the show was supposed to start, I began to panic and decided to just knock on a total stranger's door and ask if I could watch Dylan on his television. Sounds funny to me now, but that's exactly what I did. I flew down a flight of stairs to a door where I heard loud music playing and rang the bell. The guy who answered said it would be all right on one condition—I'd have to take part in the "game" they were playing. I was ready to agree to just about anything at that point, because I really wanted to see Dylan.

He allowed me in, and I passed through a beaded curtain to find a room full of naked people. I was told I, too, would have to strip, and did so. Completely ignoring the nudists, I sat down in front of the television (in my birthday suit) and turned the channel to *The Johnny Cash Show*. Someone brought out a big paper bag filled with lots of different masks and directed me to put one on. Again, I agreed, but chose one with holes for the eyes so I could continue watching the program.

As soon as Dylan finished playing, I put my clothes back on, turned in my mask, thanked them, and left. Man, what lengths one will go to to spend an evening with Bob.

"Dylan's lyrics changed the soul of pop music from undirected adolescent rebellion, to a more focused form of expression that captured the fears and dreams of youth, and led them into battle against established corruption and injustice. His music was at the forefront of a movement that made us believe we could change the world into a better place.

—Roger McGuinn

1970

I'll Be Your Baby Tonight

Pamela Des Barres *has been called the world's most famous groupie because of her delightful, best-selling book* I'm with the Band: Confessions of a Groupie, *[1987, William Morrow]. She has also written* Take Another Little Piece of My Heart: A Groupie Grows Up *and* Rock Bottom: Dark Moments in Music Babylon. *She can be reached through her web site at* http://electricgypsy.com/pamela/. *Portions of this piece have been excerpted with permission from* Take Another Little Piece of My Heart.

I really don't remember the first time I heard a Bob Dylan song, but it was at a time in my life when it seemed like something amazing happened every day. My friend Victor Hayden [Captain Beefheart's cousin] turned me on to Dylan's first album in 1964, right after I'd first heard the Beatles. I remember that hat he wore on the cover.

The first thing I thought when I heard his voice was "I've found a God." He was speaking my language, saying all the things I felt before I could put them into words. He did that for me right from the beginning. Then, when I heard his electric music, it was like he put it all together for me. I got to see him at the Santa Monica Civic Center on the 1965 tour where he went electric. He wore a herringbone suit. I was taking a

Patti D'Arbanville

Pamela Des Barres and Bob Dylan.

photography class at the time and have photos of that show. They're a bit blurry, but they're great.

Once, around 1965, I saw him on the Sunset Strip. He was leaning against a coffee house, smoking a cigarette, and wearing those pegged pants and that wild hair of his. I thought I would die. He was the epitome of coolness, and he knew it. Dylan knew way too much, and I kept waiting for him to dole it out to me so I could know too much, too. I made it a goal to acquire that sort of knowledge. For me, it was more about feeling than intellect, but Dylan combined the two. God, it was just awesome.

I always thought Bob was incredibly devastating looking. He had those cheekbones, that out-of-control hair, and those piercing know-it-all eyes. He was so slim. And the way he held himself, the look on his face...please! I still find Dylan devastatingly handsome, but he represents so much more than a physical thing to me. I'd marry Bob Dylan tomorrow. No question about it. He's done so much for me in my life.

The first time I met him was around 1970, at a Waylon Jennings show at the Troubadour. Willie Nelson introduced us, and Bob gave me a wet-fish handshake while I gazed at his Ray-Bans in the dark. I stood there hopefully in my garter belt for a few lonely moments while he looked off into the murky distance, but I suppose he didn't feel like chatting. I had finally met Bob Dylan, and he didn't give a shit.

It was 17 years before I got another chance. My friend Joycie had a little party at a cool soul-food joint on Pico, and she invited Bob. I'd gotten over just about everybody and met almost everyone I wanted to meet except for Stephen King and Prince. It took a long time, but I finally realized all my heroes are silly, insecure human goofballs just like me. What a relief. Still, no one on the planet inspired me the way Bob Dylan has, so I was happy to be in the same room with him again.

When we were introduced, I got a handful of damp fish once more and assumed that the wimpy pompano was a form of protection from getting too many people in his face. Since it was more like good-bye than hello, I started dancing to some Motown, and when I dance I lose my mind. It's my form of meditation and I go O-U-T. So imagine my surprise when I came back down to earth and Bob Dylan was standing in front of me, watching. "Do you want to dance?" I asked before I could think about it too hard. He grinned from inside his shades and encircled me from behind, where he hung on for 30 minutes. It took a couple of songs by the Temptations and one by the Four Tops before I got adjusted to his sense of rhythm, which was as jarring and jangling as his lyrics. Yes, dolls, time stopped. But because I had recently become friends with his girlfriend, Carole, I didn't even have the old flirtation temptation. He did say one of the best things that's ever been said to me, however. He asked what I did for a living. I told him I was a writer, and he said, "What else do you do? I can think of 20 or 30 things I'd like to do with you." He stepped back and studied me. "Yes, you could take you anywhere." Wow. What a compliment.

Several months later, I was invited to his birthday party. I felt like I had won first prize on the planet. What could be more divine than helping my hero celebrate his day of birth? What do you get Bob Dylan for his birthday, anyway? What becomes a legend most? Another black leather vest? I spent two entire days traipsing all around town, attempting to procure the perfect trinket. I wound up with an antique copper ashtray painted with real berries and grasses and hand-beaten by an entire tribe of Indians. At least that's what the *trés chic* salesperson told me. She was wearing some sort of authentic-looking buckskin getup with several old Indian-head nickels down the front, so who knows? They wrapped the important artifact in unbleached muslin and tied it with raffia. I wrote something on the card about lifelong inspiration, trying real hard not to kiss his ass too proudly. You can tell he's real sick of it.

We got to Bob's house on time, and the roosters scattered and the dust flew. It was so ramshackle on the outside, it must have been designed to keep out prying eyes. But after wading through the chicken coops, yakking ducks, heaps of old wood, cages, and rubbish, it was like pulling back the Technicolor curtain to the land of Oz. Lush green all around a gigantic glass-and-wood abode, with the shimmering ocean as a backdrop.

The first person I ran into was Roy Orbison, all in black with serious sunglasses. Hmm, there's Tom Petty, Jeff Lynne, Debra Winger, Joycie, Carole, various cool musicians, hip record-business types, George Harrison...GEORGE HARRISON! So, Bob calls my friend Patti [D'Arbanville] and I over to embrace us, and we sit down with him under a big umbrella. Dogs woof, children laugh, the sun glints and sparkles on the sea. It's Bob's birthday, and it's all too perfect. He introduces us to George; we are pink-cheeked and starry-eyed. "Oh, we've met a couple of times, haven't we?" George said to me. Did he remember me sinking into the blacktop at A&M Records back in '69? The brief moment in the recording studio with that nutty friend of mine a couple years ago? "Bob, have you read that wonderful book of Pamela's? I'm not in it...unfortunately." He laughed and told Patti that she was a legend, and she said, "Look who's talking."

It was a bit overwhelming, all very charming and tra-la. Bob leaned over to me and said, "Maybe we could work together on a screenplay or something." I grinned the rest of the day and well into the star-filled Malibu night, dancing to cool old songs on the cool old jukebox that George, Jeff, and Tom had gotten Bob for his birthday. None of the brilliant, creative souls at the party could figure out how to hook the thing up at first. Bob stood by watching with his arms crossed saying, "Don't look at me." But Tom finally plugged it in, and everybody cheered. Bob seemed to enjoy his jukebox, but I didn't get to see him open the other gifts, so I don't know how the hand-beaten, berry-stained ashtray went over. I hope he liked it.

Today, I go to his concerts every couple of years. A year and a half ago, E! Entertainment Network (I work for them) sent me to Minneapolis, and I reviewed him there. I wanted to be in his home state to see how the people reacted to him. Needless to say, I gave him a rave review. The audience was fascinating, with people of all ages and types, including 18-year-olds who knew every word to every song. It was fantastic. Dylan just crosses all boundaries.

I tried to get backstage but was unsuccessful that time. Right around the time of his birthday party, he put me on the backstage list, and I got to talk with him. At that point, I really thought that I was going to become a friend, because of the way he was acting toward me. He said he wanted to write a screenplay with me. He seemed to dig me. We had an amazing rapport there. But who knows? He may just make those sort of connections with people, and then they're over. He called me once, and I missed his call because I was at the gym. I called my house and asked my assistant if I had any messages. She said, "No, no messages. Oh, wait. Bob Dylan called." I said, "Did he leave a number?" She said, "No, he didn't. He said he'd call back." He never did. That call came a week after he said we'd get together to talk about the screenplay.

I just finished that screenplay, by the way. So I've been thinking now that I know how to write one, I should get in touch with Bob and let him know I've actually completed one. It's about James Dean. Through my research, I've become best friends with all his family and friends. I never do things halfway in my life.

My Back Pages

Rob Stoner *was Bob Dylan's bassist and bandleader from 1975 to 1979, an era that encompassed the Rolling Thunder Revue and the* Desire, Hard Rain, Live at Budokan, *and* Biograph *albums. He has also toured and recorded with Don McLean, Robert Gordon, and Link Wray; appeared on hundreds of albums as a studio musician; and released solo albums on Epic, MCA, and Sun. Since 1995, he has performed a one-man all-star show.*

I first met Bob in 1971, when I played the Ash Grove folk club in L.A. with a guy named John Herald. John is an interesting guy who Dylan would come to see when he was in town. He was the leader of a bluegrass band called the Greenbriar Boys, who were the headliners on the night that Robert Shelton wrote the famous *New York Times* review that put Bob on the map.

After the gig, we went back to the Sunset Hotel and hung out all night. It was a little intimidating at first, because I was a fan. But basically, I was just excited, because I was thinking, "He's going to need somebody someday, and when he does, he'll probably call." And sure enough, a few years later he did. That's the way things go in the music business, at least it used to anyway; one person leads to another.

Walter Beckham

Dylan and Rob Stoner, Rolling Thunder Revue, 1976.

Musicians are always scouting for potential future players—people they can make a substitute move with eventually. They're looking for people who sound good and are personally simpatico, and that's one of the reasons we hung out all night. He just wanted to see if he could stand me. Personality matches are at least as important as talent. Better to have somebody you can stand being around than some superior player who's an asshole.

How long was it before you met again?

A couple of years. I was back in L.A. in 1973, and we hung out together a bit then. Then I saw him again in the summer of 1975, at the Other End in Greenwich Village. *Blood on the Tracks* was a success at the time, and there was a little scene going on there where Bob would sit in with people like Ramblin' Jack Elliott and Bob Neuwirth. I had my own band at the time, but I'd also been working with Jack some and hanging out in the Village.

He'd started to work on what became the *Desire* album around then, but was having a hard time. One night, he and his producer came to see someone at the Other End, probably Jack, and I ran into them there. They asked me to come to the next night's session and tell them what I thought. When I got there, I found they were trying to do a superstar session thing, and it wasn't working. They had Dave Mason, Eric Clapton, Emmylou Harris, Scarlett Rivera, and an eight-piece band named Kokomo. And all kinds of people were just hanging out.

I suggested they get rid of all the extra people and use the smallest band possible. Bob's music depends on catching a moment, and he hates to record a song more than a couple of times. All those people were complicating things, and nothing was getting done. He kept Emmylou and Scarlett, I got Howie Wyeth to come in on drums, and we finished the album in a couple of nights.

How did that lead to the Rolling Thunder Revue?

I think Bob started getting the urge to tour again around then. I got a call about a week after we did the album, saying that he wanted the same group to do the John Hammond TV Special with him in Chicago. That was my first live gig with him, and it was kind of a tryout for the band. When he decided to put Rolling Thunder together, Scarlett, Howie, and I were the core band.

The whole idea of the Rolling Thunder Revue was that most of the people in the band were singer/songwriters in their own right, like Mick Ronson and T-Bone Burnett. We'd all be the opening act and play for about an hour before Dylan even came onstage. The back-up band would do about an hour, and then Joan would come out and do a half an hour or so. Then Roger McGuinn would do a turn, and someone else would do a half-hour after him. We'd take an intermission and each one of them would come out again. Before you knew it, four hours had passed. That was the format of the show.

Why do you think Bob chose to include Bobby Neuwirth on the tour and make him the leader?

I think it was Dylan's payback for all that Neuwirth had done for him in the past. Before Bob was anybody, Neuwirth was supposedly one of the "original Bobs." Neuwirth was on a folk-singing trip up around Cambridge before Bob had his act together. Also, it showed off some of Dylan's roots, as if Bob was saying, "Here are the people that influenced me; I'm bringing them along." That's why Ramblin' Jack was there. It was sort of like a Bob Dylan museum.

Another reason Neuwirth was given the Rolling Thunder leadership was that he was such a witty guy, a clever turner of phrases. Dylan knew this, and a lot of the things that ended up in Bob's songs were "Neuwirthisms." For instance, "Don't look back" was always a credo of Neuwirth's. It makes a lot of sense; they were on the road together 24 hours a day for years during the period when Dylan was coming up with all of that material that later became some of his most famous stuff.

Even Dylan's mom, Beattie, was on the tour, wasn't she?

Yep, Dylan invited her. I've got pictures of us together. I think she was there mostly as a buffer between Bob and Sara. They were fighting, and in the process of breaking up. Having Beattie along kept Sara from causing a scene. She helped look after the kids, that sort of thing. I could see that the marriage was definitely going to be over. I met Sara one of the first times that I met Bob again back in '75, when I was doing the *Desire* album, and I could see the vibe. She seemed like she wasn't ready to accept the fact that he was ready to move on.

Were there a lot of groupies around?

Oh. yeah. It was the '70s, and those were the golden days before the scary stuff. It was still the era of free love. At that point, Bob already had a bunch of kids with Sara and was realizing that he wasn't ready to settle down yet, even though he'd already created a family. Sara was being kind of demanding about it. By going on the road, Bob realized that the gypsy lifestyle was for him, and he started getting back into it. He was in his thirties and feeling like he was in his twenties, and he and Sara just had a parting of the ways. He had gotten together with Sara to raise a family when he was pretty inactive musically. Then he started feeling the call of the road again, and it became an incompatible thing with them.

What was your experience like making the film Renaldo and Clara?

It was a gas making that film, even though it turned out a bit disjointed. But considering that everyone involved had never made a film before, it wasn't bad. It wasn't *that* far from Fellini. Obviously, the tech people and the editors had been involved in filmmaking before, but Bob was in charge. It was his bread.

Did you make it to the premiere?

Yeah, sure did, but I was so caught up in the excitement of being an "actor in a movie" at a Hollywood premiere that I couldn't tell what the reaction was. There were some really stupid technical mishaps, though. We were rehearsing the afternoon of the premiere in Santa Monica when a bunch of guys came running in and interrupted the rehearsals saying, "Bob, this theater doesn't have stereo or Dolby or anything, and the P.A. system is just a couple of speakers up in the curtain." Back in those days, they didn't have all these state-of-the-art theater sound systems, and they had to scramble to put a P.A. in there at the last minute, so that the concert sections would sound big.

Does that last-minute stuff stress Dylan?

Nah, but he wouldn't have shown it even if it did. Bob sometimes appears to be stressed, but he's not. He's just got a lot of stuff simultaneously going on in his mind.

Did you ever see Bob make personal contact with his fans when you toured with him?

All the time—in lobbies, outside shows, and in the local music scene, like at nightclubs and music stores. When I was hanging out with him, he always liked to mingle and blow people's minds. The only way you can really find out what's going on without people "yessing" you is to go out and actually talk to the fans. They were always flabbergasted. "Wow, it's really *him*." I hear he's still like that.

He doesn't go looking for them; the fans find *him*. They know where you're going to stay. Dylan fans always scout that stuff out. We used to have people follow us around for entire tours.

Did you ever see a fan try to harm Bob in any way?

I never saw a fan who deliberately tried to harm him. There were a couple of times when Bob might have been in harm's way from the kind of shit that happens in crowds when people are all jammed together towards the front and standing there for a long time. You know, where somebody steps on someone else's foot or jostles somebody else's chick, and things get ornery.

Sid Vicious was the only person I ever saw threaten Bob. They both were at a London gig I played with Robert Gordon in 1979, and Sid came backstage after our first set and started waving a knife around the room and hassling Bob, just being a drunken asshole. He was saying, "Hey, you're Bob Dildo then, aren't you? Eh! Fuck you, Bob Dildo." Bob asked me, "Rob, who *is* this guy?" He wasn't freaked or anything. Bob boxes; he's a tough little guy and can take care of himself. We just grabbed Sid and hustled him out of the room.

Did you ever see Bob's temper flare?

Yeah, sure, but no more than anybody else. Sometimes, he'd just get impatient with stuff, and he'd come to me and say, "Hey, man, I wish I could just go out there and do my show. That would be enough to worry about, but I got all this other shit to deal with all the time."

Isn't that why he hires managers?

Yeah, but it still comes down to him. They can handle some of it for him, but the real decisions have to made by Bob. He has to tell them what to do. When something goes down, it weighs on the guy's mind, even though somebody else is taking care of it for him. One of my functions was to be a buffer with the musicians, so he wouldn't have to deal with the daily nuts and bolts stuff of leading a band. I was the bandleader, and it was my job to deal with all the stuff that I knew Bob didn't want to be bothered with; stupid stuff like, "Oh man, let me have a guitar solo tonight." I didn't want them to be hassling Bob about such trivial shit, because he always had enough on his mind.

When did you quit working for Bob?

He put a tour together to go to Japan and Australia in late 1978, and I was in charge of that. I cut loose from that tour in early '79, just as he was getting into the "Gotta Serve Somebody" Christian mode. It wasn't because I didn't want to play that music, because I think everything he's done is great. It was just time for me to do something different. He's one of a kind...he's Bob Dylan. They don't call him a legend for nothing, man.

What is it for you that makes Dylan so brilliant?

His presence. He's just got this *je ne sais quois*, this charismatic thing going on. With those steel-blue eyes and his magnetism, I swear the guy could persuade anyone to do almost anything. Plus, the guy's a genius; he's got an amazing mind.

1973

Wedding Song

Ruggero Santacroce

Born in 1942, a year later than Bob Dylan, I was a boy coming from Elvis' big experience. As a teenager, I was a great fan of Elvis, the Everly Brothers, and Fats Domino. It was the birth of Rock and Roll.

In 1966 I married a beautiful girl named Lelia. She was a true Christian, full of deep, genuine faith I was unable to understand. Like me, she was a Socialist. But I was (and still am) an agnostic, and this difference caused some troubles in our marriage. Still, between 1967 and 1972, we had three daughters and a son. As Dylan sings in "Wedding Song":

You gave me babies one, two, three. What's more, you saved my life.

During those years, I was very committed to my career in marketing research and to being a father and husband. Music, which had been a very important part of my life, was almost abandoned.

In 1973, Lelia, then 32, was diagnosed with cancer. The doctors tried to operate but were unsuccessful. On the July 14, 1973, my beautiful wife died in my arms. I followed her last, lost look from the glow of the lamp in her room and watched her take her last breath.

It was difficult to survive; I was so young and inexperienced, and it was just too hard to handle. I constantly thought about Lelia. There were so many things unresolved between us, so many things to tell and ask her, knowing that I would receive no answers. I had to give my children the impossible news and inflict this terrible pain. Imagine my trouble and desperation.

While on a short holiday at the sea with two of my children in August 1973, I wandered into a shop where I found a book called *Bob Dylan: Blues, Ballads and Songs*. It contained the words to most of his songs from 1961-1970, translated into Italian. I read it in just a few days, thinking, "This man has fiery blood in his veins." At last I knew all the words to "All Along the Watchtower."

Let us not talk falsely now, the hour is getting late.

We headed back to Milan a few days later, where I bought all of Dylan's records. In the long, dark nights of desperation over the following months, I became intimately connected with Bob's songs and, in truth, probably survived because of him. Around this time I wrote a poem for Lelia, with Bob's spirit influencing me. Reading it 25 years later, I notice its sentiments echo the words Bob sings in "Love Sick."

I see silhouettes in the windows, I watch them till they're gone, and they leave me hanging on...to a shadow.

And my consciousness expanded. Though I was in a very fragile state of mind, I found I was being touched "by the grace." It's so difficult to say how, but I was helped by Bob's beautiful words again and again. I began listening to "Hard Rain," "Tomorrow is a Long Time," "Blowin' in the Wind," and "One Too Many Mornings," feeling that light wind of the spirit that refreshes and enlivens everything. I was going deeply into the words and expressions. I soon realized that Bob Dylan was a poet, deeply involved in what I call the "poetry of life." Good and bad things happen, and the job of the poet is to expand consciousness (wonderful and splendid mission that it is). It was in this way that the never-ending story of Bob Dylan and I began.

The first time I saw him live and in concert was in 1978, in Nuremberg and Paris. Since then, I've seen him every time he's come to Italy. In June of 1989, Bob played Palatrussardi here in Milan during the Never Ending Tour. Despite security, I went close to the stage to take pictures of my hero, where he was singing a magnificent version of "Shelter From the Storm."

I'm living in a foreign country, but I'm bound to cross the line, beauty walks a razor's edge, someday I'll make it mine.

On the CD of this show, during the silence after the song, you can hear a man shouting "Poeta!" I am that man, giving my personal Nobel Prize to Bob.

As I listen to Dylan's album *Time Out of Mind*, it seems as if we are walking down the same path in life: *Got to sleep down in the parlor and relive my dreams.*

Yes, of course, it is the same path. Thank you, Bob Dylan. Please, everyone, if you see him, say hello. He might be in your dreams.

"Bob Dylan is a talented artist who has long been a kind of hero to me. I first became aware of his music many years ago when my sons bought all his albums. During my term as governor of Georgia, I invited Dylan to perform at the Governor's Mansion. I'll always remember that incredible performance and the intimate talk he and I shared that evening. His music is simple yet moving. Even today, whenever he's in Georgia, I always try to attend his concerts."

—*former President Jimmy Carter*

Minstrel Boy

David Grisman *is the world's preeminent mandolinist. With a unique blend of jazz, classical, bluegrass, and ethnic music, his 1977 release,* The David Grisman Quintet *[Rhino], completely redefined the parameters of instrumental acoustic string bands and launched a new musical genre. His music has continued to evolve as he tours and records with his current band. He can be reached through his web site at* www.dawgnet.com.

Though we were there at the same time, and played in some of the same clubs, I didn't know Bob Dylan in the Village. I used to see him around on the street, but I didn't really appreciate that singer/songwriter sort of music then. To me, they were just singing songs and not tuning their guitars. I was into the *real* folk musicians, like Clarence Ashley, Roscoe Holcomb, and Doc Watson.

My first real contact with him was in 1974, when he called me out of the blue for some mandolin lessons. I didn't really believe it was him on the phone. It sounded like him, but I'd never met the guy. A half-hour later, he was on my back porch with a blonde Gibson F-4. He stayed for

David Grisman and Bill Monroe, 1977.

three days and then disappeared. Bob was a fine student, but he wasn't that interested in the technical stuff. I showed him some basic fingering and some chords, but I think he just wanted to learn how to write a song on the mandolin. He was interested in bluegrass music and all the other stuff that I was into, so we mostly just listened to records and hung out. I charged him $15.00 a day for the lessons, and he still owes me $3.00.

The next week, my band opened for Bill Monroe at the Palomino Club in Los Angeles. Dylan was real interested in Bill, so I'd told him about the gig. So here we are, playing our new music at a gig opening for Bill Monroe. After our set—Bill had come in after we started—I was out in the parking lot and [violinist] Richard Greene came out and said, "I just saw Bill Monroe, and he ignored me. I stood next to him for 10 minutes, and he didn't acknowledge my existence." See, not only had Richard played in Bill's band, but Bill had always praised him. But this night, he was giving Richard the cold shoulder.

I said, "Well, he's not gonna do that to me." We were tight; he used to call me up onstage; I named my son Monroe Grisman. He was into me when I was playing successor to the throne, but I wasn't so sure how he'd be now that I wasn't playing just bluegrass. So I went inside, and I'm standing in the doorway to the dressing room, wondering if I should go say hello or what, and all of a sudden who shows up but Dylan and

Robbie Robertson. Bob says, "I really dug the set. Hey, I want to meet the man!" So, here I am about to be possibly snubbed by Bill, and I have to introduce Bob Dylan to him. Suddenly, Bill turns toward me, sticks out his hand, and smiles. He was real impressed when I introduced Dylan to him; they sang "I Saw the Light" together backstage.

Somewhere around 1981, I was playing a gig in Portland, Oregon. We'd come in the night before and found out that Dylan was playing at the Portland Paramount. Craig Miller, my manager, knew Bob's road manager, and I knew Jim Keltner, who was drumming with Dylan. So, Craig talked to Bob's road manager and got us all tickets to the show. We go down there and get to the box office, and the minute I showed up, someone approached me and said, "Mr. Grisman, Mr. Dylan would like to see you in his dressing room." They immediately ushered me in, took me backstage, and deposited me in an empty dressing room.

A couple of minutes later, Bob showed up. We talked a bit, and then he excused himself for a minute and went out. Before I knew it, a security guy came in and said, "What are you doing here?" I told him that Bob had invited me, but he didn't believe me and made me leave. During the show, Bob mentioned that there was this really fine musician in the audience that he'd wanted to ask to play, but that he'd disappeared from his dressing room before he'd had the chance. Then he mentioned my name. I didn't really do anything about it, but about 10 minutes later an usher found me and said, "Come on backstage. Bob wants you to play." So, I went back, and they got me out onstage when the next number finished. I guess he had a musician who played mandolin because there was one leaning against an amp. I picked it up and spent half the song trying to tune the thing.

That's the only time I ever played with Bob onstage. He's kind of a mystery guy; he crops up in different places and then disappears just as fast. Like one time I had a gig in a famous jazz club down in southern California called the Lighthouse. When we showed up to load in our equipment in the afternoon, Bob was sitting there at the bar with his wife, sort of waiting for us. He said, "Hi, good to see you." After we loaded in our stuff, we had to check into our hotel. When we came back, he was gone. Strange stuff.

1974

Driftin' Too Far from the Shore

Radha Damodas *(née Donald Delaney) has been a Dylan fan since age 16. On his 20th birthday, he renounced "his moraless hippie life" and joined the Hare Krisha Temple in Victoria, British Columbia. Now 48, he lives in a Northern Florida community of 500 Hare Krishna devotees, where they farm and home-school their children.*

I've been a Hare Krishna devotee since 1971, and in 1974 I was part of the Denver Temple, where I distributed religious literature and collected donations in public places daily. Several of the Target department stores in the area allowed devotees to preach and distribute pamphlets near the entrances.

One fall day I was distributing literature in front of the Target store wearing the standard orange robe and sporting the shaved head of a single (or monastic) student. I had my requisite box of small Krishna books and magazines, and around noon, I telephoned the Temple to report in. The Temple President came on the line.

"Radha," he exclaimed, "Bob Dylan was just here. He walked right into the Temple room looking like he'd just stepped off an album cover, complete with curly hair and dusty jeans."

His voice was a mixture of excitement and disbelief. "He didn't talk to anyone," he continued. "Just chanted on his prayer beads for about

Radha Damodas, 1974.

two hours while his traveling companions and his wife gathered up all the spiritual vegetarian foods they could find. They also went to the gift store and the book warehouse, where they bought up everything they could carry, like books, posters, and incense."

He told me Dylan was good friends with George Harrison of the Beatles, who I knew was a devotee. Harrison had apparently influenced Bob to check out the practice of Krishna's service. One of our great leaders, Puspa Dasa, had traveled from New York to Los Angeles in Dylan's van with some of Bob's musicians, teaching them about Krishna as they crossed the country.

About 15 minutes after my phone call, I was back distributing books by the Target store when I saw Puspa Dasa himself walking across the parking lot and headed my way.

"Bob Dylan is out in the parking lot and would like to speak with you," he said. Nervously, I picked up my box of literature and followed him.

As I entered the van, I saw Dylan sitting on the floorboard strumming his guitar, which had a photograph of Krishna on the body and another of our spiritual Master A.C. Bhaktivedanta Swami on the neck. Taped to the walls of the van were pictures that appeared to have been torn from our monthly magazine *Back to Godhead*.

"Please, come in," Bob said softly. "Sit down...have some Prasadam [vegetarian holy food]."

The couple in the front of the van hurried about preparing a large spread of Prepasatione (milk, fruit, bread, etc., from the Temple). As I ate,

I tried to overcome my anxiety by politely telling Bob how nice it was that he'd taken to the beautiful teachings of Krishna. Dylan nodded his head in solemn agreement. He seemed incredibly shy and withdrawn, constantly strumming his guitar.

"Hey Bob, let's sing him the song you just wrote called 'Come to Krishna'," Puspa Dasa exclaimed.

Bob again nodded his head, and they all grabbed small instruments and began singing a lively song with the chorus: "Come to Krishna, come to Krishna, Come to Krishna, Hari-Bol." ("Hari-Bol" means to constantly chant holy names.)

Unfortunately, he sang so softly and strummed so loudly that I couldn't make out the other lyrics. After the song, I picked up my literature, thanked them all for their hospitality, and headed back to the Target store to continue spreading the word about Krishna.

Later, I read in our monthly newsletter, *The Iskon World Review*, that Dylan had also visited the Temple of Krishna in Los Angeles, where he left a small velvet bag filled with jewels on the altar.

I often wonder what became of his song I heard in his van that fall day in 1974. "Come to Krishna" would sure be a boost for Hare Krishnas everywhere, should he ever decide to record it.

1974

Went to See the Gypsy

Rudy J. Miera, *46, is a public school teacher in Albuquerque, New Mexico, and a teacher consultant with the National Writing Project based in Berkeley, California. A Dylan fan since high school, he is currently working on several screenplays and teaching himself to play charango and Bajo Sexto.*

Unfortunately, the predictions had come true. It was 1974, and the nation had been gripped by the icy jaws of subarctic temperatures for long months with more wild winter expected. Because of the Arab oil embargo, gasoline was being rationed and pumps were running only a few hours each day. Then, in the midst of this darkness, came an unexpected light: Bob Dylan and The Band announced a plan to tour the United States.

In high school, I got caught up with Dylan, appreciating and decoding those classic albums a few years after they had been released. But it wasn't until my junior and senior years at Valley High, from '69 through '71, that I traveled in depth through the "smoky rings" of the poetic caverns of *Highway 61 Revisited* and *Blonde on Blonde*. Then, in a full-page ad in the Sunday *Denver Post*, the incredible report was verified. My chance to see Bob Dylan in the flesh, singing those romantically prophetic and poetic tales, was a possibility.

Somehow, I managed to convince a couple of close friends that the journey from Albuquerque to Denver in the midst of the worst winter in our young lives wasn't going to be that difficult. After all, the man was/is a legend. What was undeniably a challenge to my patience, though, was after sending in money orders (at nearly $20.00 a ticket, the most I'd ever paid to see a live musician), we had to wait for a lottery to see if we would be allowed to buy them. Nothing was guaranteed. So we waited...and waited...and waited....and gave up. At least I did; it had been more than a month since our letter to Bill Graham Presents at a Colorado post office box. In fact, I was pretty angry at Mr. Graham for getting my hopes up and ripping me off.

One night, totally unexpectedly, I dreamed our tickets were in the mail. The next day I walked out into the cold, gray morning to the mailbox and found my self-addressed, stamped envelope with three beautiful tickets inside.

On the day we set out for Denver, I remember waiting for the gas attendant and thinking that he might not even come to open up. Gas rationing, remember? Would we be stuck halfway there? We later found ourselves parked in a lot in the dark early morning before sunrise, somewhere near the New Mexico-Colorado border. About once an hour we'd start the old, white Plymouth Valiant and let the engine run long enough to power the whistling heater that melted the ice on the windows (and ourselves), then drift off for another 50-minute arctic nap.

Finally, at sunset on February 6th, we pulled into the jammed parking lot of the Denver Coliseum, where the afternoon show had just let out. Amidst a surreal maxi-orchestra of automobile tape players simultaneously cranking out Bob Dylan's greatest hits, we confirmed our expectations with the departing concert-goers.

"Yes, he's doing 'Blowin' in the Wind' electric, and it's great," they reported. "'Lay Lady Lay' is superfast. His voice is sooo strong." After hearing the early reports and deciding where we'd park on return, we left for a short, hot supper.

Our seats were way in the back, but it didn't matter. It would only be minutes until...the lights went out, and the crowd roared like extras at the Ben-Hur chariot race. You can never be totally prepared for the arrival of a legend.

That voice. The fury and melodic electricity, nervous energy channeled into vocal prophetic yells. Oh, we had read all about Bob's "new singing style" in *Time, Newsweek,* and *Rolling Stone,* but the shock of the new was now deep and thorough. Hearing those songs we'd been growing up with, growing into, and growing out of, charged with such soulful joy and fear, sent shivers up and down the spines of the thousands of winter pilgrims huddled for a couple hours' shelter from the storm. The quick parade of resurrected sonic moods and impressions was over all too quickly, and The Band then took us on a collective ride through the back roads of late 20th-Century North America.

I didn't drive that far on ice and snow not to see the man closer. After the acoustic set, I left my seat and walked the length of the Coliseum to the area behind Dylan's side of the stage. After the astonishing celebrations of "Highway 61 Revisited" and "Like a Rolling Stone," with house lights on reflecting triumph on the faces of performer and witnesses, he came, he saw, he conquered, and he left.

And then he came back again. Once more, the cavernous, pilgrim-filled Coliseum was shaken by the amplified generation's voice of fury and hope. A quick two-song encore, a soulful reprise of "Most Likely You Go Your Way (and I'll Go Mine)," and an electric "Blowin' in the Wind," all on our feet, feeling the earthshaking spontaneous cry of celebration and applause in full naked light. Brother Bob took it all in, turned around, then walked down the several steps below us on our side of the stage. The screaming and yelling from those around me rising above the other sections caught his ear. He looked up smiling, and the 20-something girl next to me yelled out, *"Bob."* He grabbed the white towel from around his neck and tossed it up at her. The rapt attentions of thousands in ecstasy were focused on him.

Have you ever been in a crowd of people howling and screaming so loud that there is this temporary, pure white silence? Where time itself is hooked, held in its tracks by the power of the crowd? In that pocket of quiet, distracted time, I reached into my green army jacket and pulled out the folded sheets of poems I'd been working on. My mind curiously watched my hand reach into the large pocket and fling the small packet of folded paper up onto the stage, where it bounced off Dylan's shoulder. Then, Bob did the impossible. He bent down, picked up my papers, put them in his pocket, and vanished backstage.

Whoosh! The smells, pandemonium, and chaos surrounded us again, and I couldn't move. "Will he read those fragmented poems now or later?" I thought to myself. "Will they spark a work-scheme in his mind, evolve into an idea, complete a thought?" This had been a youth-topia, slow-motion dream as the outside world aged.

The much-anticipated masterpiece *Blood On The Tracks* appeared slightly more than a year later, returning a penny-arcade spirit of possibilities to the time-encrusted planet. I remember the moment I first heard a 50-second flash from "Idiot Wind," at the corners of Yale and Coal streets as the late-afternoon gray traffic crawled through the after-rain. That series of tumbling images sung with such passion. It was personal drama captured into words; true cinema for the ears and imagination. What a brilliant, illuminating series of song dramas. What a deeply passionate record of life's disillusionments. And, no, there couldn't be any rhyme-schemes or anything remotely related to those half-songs on those folded bits of paper I'd thrown at the concert a year before...could there? Certain phrases *did* seem to echo. That sonic ecstasy of the gypsy's condemnation of the lonely road was the soundtrack to my life for the next few college, starving-artist years.

Many winters have come and gone since that freeze-breaking, 1974 Dylan show. In fact, over half of my life has been lived since. Now I write, teach, sometimes pick up my guitar, and even write movies. Still, every early Spring, I am reminded by one song or another of the first time I saw Bob Dylan in concert. What a dream it was...what a dream it is.

Trouble in Mind

Lawrence Morrissey, *45, has been a Dylan fan since the release of* Another Side *in 1964. "It was the first album I ever purchased, and it's one of my favorites to this day. I like to write songs while riding my bicycle and play guitar."*

I t was at the 1974 Friends of Chile concert at New York City's Felt Forum when I first encountered Bob Dylan. Because we're both Dylan freaks, my girlfriend and I decided to try to catch a glimpse of him outside the stage door after the show.

While standing near the door, we noticed a commotion about a block down the street. Curiosity got the best of us, and we headed toward the source, only to find Dylan himself slouched against a concrete flowerpot and muttering to himself. After a few moments, his friends arrived, happy to have found him.

Apparently, he'd wandered away from the group, which included Dennis Hopper, Phil Ochs, and Daniel Ellsberg. Everyone was just kind of hanging around the flowerpot when someone realized that Dylan had left his guitar unattended back in the dressing room and tore off to fetch it. Bob kept saying, over and over, "My guitar. My guitar. What would I do without my guitar?" This brought laughter from his friends.

Just then Dylan dropped a vest he'd been clutching underneath his brown-leather bomber jacket. As he bent down to retrieve it, some jerk ran by and stole the cap off his head. Dylan stood straight up, grabbed his head, and began screaming, "My hat. He took my hat."

Realizing what had happened, I dashed off after the thief. During my pursuit, I noticed Dennis Hopper running behind me. I cornered the kid in a doorway and coerced him into returning the hat. As the kid ran off into the night, Hopper approached and said, "Hey, that was pretty cool what you just did. Why don't you come to the after-show party?"

He gave me the address of a building on Central Park West, and I agreed to join them. Then I returned to get my girlfriend and see what else was happening at the flowerpot. Dylan and Ochs had just commandeered a taxicab to take them to the party, and things got a little crazy at this point as everyone but us piled into the cab.

Somehow, they managed to get all their guitars and girlfriends inside and close the doors, but the cab just sat there. After a few seconds, the doors swung open and the cabdriver threw them all out, complaining that he couldn't see out the back window. Dylan got violently angry and began punching the driver's side window with all his might, screaming, "*You mother——,*" over and over. He was literally beating up the fellow's cab and cursing like a streetperson, and I know what that is when I hear it.

My girl and I decided to drive uptown to the party to see what would happen next. As we entered the vestibule of a very swanky apartment complex, we were greeted by a doorman. After determining our destination, he asked if we would mind waiting until the next couple came out, due to overcrowding. We didn't mind at all, and after 15 minutes or so, we were admitted to the apartment and led into a room with walls lined with silver foil. Surrounded by people, Dylan and his wife, Sara, stood in the center, drinking and talking.

Soon after we walked in, Sara came up to me and asked for a cigarette, the first of 10 she'd bum off me that night. In fact, she bummed so many that Bob began to look a bit embarrassed by it. He also seemed embarrassed that Sara kept jumping in front of him while he was in the midst of conversation with someone, saying things like, "Look, Bob. There's

Phil Ochs over there. He told me that he wants to talk with you." She did it so often that Dylan began to ignore her completely and continued chatting with his friends. As the evening wore on, he appeared more relaxed and charming, and it was hard to believe that only a few hours earlier he'd beat up on a taxicab, cursed the driver, and created a scene for the whole world to see.

While wandering around, we strolled into what we later learned was the "older people's" room. It featured an open bar and many distinguished looking men in tuxedos. Looking and feeling a bit out of place, we were directed to the "young people's" room, where I soon found myself standing at the bar next to Dennis Hopper. We poured each other many drinks that magical night in New York City.

Later, as I wandered out of the bar area in search of my girlfriend, I spotted Dylan shouting at a young girl in one of the side rooms. He was waving his finger in her face saying, "I can tell what you want...money. That's what you want. It's money, right? I can see right through you."

The girl, obviously very embarrassed, just smiled and sat down. Hours later, we were told by the organizer of the party that the girl had been ejected from the apartment for allegedly trying to walk out with someone's purse. Apparently, Dylan somehow intuitively knew just what her game was.

As the party was breaking up, I overheard a fellow tell Bob that the car was coming around to pick him up. My girl and I ran out to our own car with the intention of intercepting the limo. We followed it to a townhouse on 64th Street, but when we tried to enter the brownstone along with the Dylan entourage, the owner stopped us at the door, saying, "You weren't with us in the limo."

I said, "That's right, but we just want to hang out for a little while."

He replied, "I'm sorry, but I can't let you in here. This is my house, so go away."

Ah well, one can always try, right? His refusal to let us join the gathering didn't dampen our evening one bit. We walked back to our car in a great mood. Our collective dream had more than come true: We'd hung out with Bob Dylan.

Driving through Queens on our way home at 8:00 A.M., everything had changed for us. We'd just left a world in Manhattan that dwarfed our own neighborhood's vitality...the world of Bob Dylan. It was then I realized I'd forgotten to return the vest I'd picked up off the sidewalk.

Incredibly, a couple of months later I encountered him again, this time at a Little Feat show at the Bottom Line. After we were seated awhile, my girlfriend said, "Hey, I think that's Bob Dylan over there." I took a better look and discovered that, indeed, it was him. So I asked our waitress to deliver a note that read, "Bob, I've got your vest. Remember the vest?"

We watched him read the note, frown, and shove it in his jeans pocket. Later, as he got up to head to the men's room, I followed him. It was a weird feeling, standing next to Bob Dylan at the urinal. So weird, in fact, that I just couldn't speak to him like I wanted to, so I said nothing. I walked out before him and ran into Allan Pepper, the owner of the Bottom Line, standing guard outside the restroom to protect Bob's privacy. Somehow, I'd managed to slip in below the radar, so to speak.

As we were heading home, I decided to drive down the street where I thought Dylan lived. I'd studied some of the Weberman photos and thought I could figure out the location. As we were driving down MacDougal Street, Dylan suddenly materialized in front of our car. I swear, I almost hit him. I could just visualize the headlines: "Near Miss of Premier Musical Poet."

Gathering our wits, we pulled up next to him, where he was just standing (rather intoxicated, it seemed) in the middle of the street. Through her open window, my girlfriend said, "Hiya, Bob, we're really big fans. Nice to see you." He mumbled something incomprehensible in response.

Slowly, I started to drive away, still shaken by our near-miss minutes earlier. I looked in the rear-view mirror, and he was still just standing there in the middle of the road. Hell, he was going to get hurt. We backed up, and I rolled down my window and asked if he needed a ride.

Chuckling, he replied, "You know, I sure could use a ride right now."

I told him to hop in, and he jammed himself and his guitar into the back seat, which was packed with my own guitars since we'd just that evening returned to the city from a two-week vacation. The entire scene seemed surreal. On the dashboard of my car were stacks of Dylan albums and my harmonica holder. In the back seat was Bob Dylan himself, squashed in amongst our dirty laundry bags.

My girlfriend immediately tried to sell me as a session musician, bragging about what a good guitar player and songwriter I was. Needless to say, I was mortified. I quickly turned around to shake his hand and tell him we'd seen him at the Bottom Line earlier that evening.

He seemed surprised and said, "Oh, you guys were there? What did you think of the show?"

I responded positively and told him that I thought Little Feat were great. "Yes, they certainly seem to know what they're doing," he agreed.

We drove a few more blocks, and he asked to be let out on Barrow Street, just past Seventh Avenue South. As he walked off into the night, he turned around and gave us a nice little wave, as if to say thanks for the ride.

1975

All I Really Want to Do

Olivia Weinstein *is a photographer and hand-coloring artist who lives in Corte Madera, California. Her work, which includes images of nature and musicians, appears in magazines and on greeting cards. She can be reached by e-mail at* visionbd@worldnet.att.net.

When I discovered Bob Dylan, I was a young poet and having a pretty hard time in my life. I used to listen to him all the time; he was like God to me, and his music saved me. So, I asked my boyfriend to help me do a painting of Dylan based on a photo in the Bangladesh booklet. He was a very good artist, and it came out really great. Of course, I told him it *had* to be great, because I was going to meet Bob and give it to him. Everyone thought I was crazy.

My uncle lived in New York's East Village, so I'd go down and stay with him. Then I'd hang out in Greenwich Village and show the painting around to people who I heard knew Bob. Eventually, I met this guy named Mike, who had a camera shop on MacDougal Street, right across from Bob's apartment. He thought the painting was really good, so he set up a meeting and told me to go to Bob's apartment at such and such a time and show it to him.

I was 18 years old and so nervous. There I was...about to meet God. My heart was pounding; I felt like I wasn't in my body. With my painting and book of poetry in hand, I rang the bell, and he answered the door. It was really dark in his apartment; there were no lights on. I could barely speak, but I gave him the painting and said, "I did this for you." I could tell he liked it, but he said, "I don't like realism. I think I'll hang it in the closet." I was going to show him some of my poetry, but I was so nervous that I dropped everything, and the papers went all over the floor. After I picked them all up, I just stood there, not saying a word. So he said, "Well, it was nice to meet you," and shook my hand and showed me to the door. I felt like such an idiot. All I could think was, "God, you blew it. There you were, alone with Bob Dylan in his apartment and you couldn't say anything." I felt terrible. A part of me felt like I just met God, and the other part of me felt so stupid. He probably thought I was an idiot.

That was right before the first Rolling Thunder Tour began, and my friend invited me to a tour kick-off party the next day at Mike's loft. I was upstairs sitting on the bed when Bob came in and sat down next to me and started talking. Again, I was so nervous that I didn't say much, but I did tell him how I wrote poetry and how my mother died when I was a little girl...stuff like that. Then he got up to do something else, and I thought I'd blown it again. When the tour kicked off a few days later, I decided I was going to follow it.

My grandmother had given me her 1963 Chevy Impala, so I drove up to Plymouth, Massachusetts, for the first show. I got there about 3:00 P.M. and went around back and found Bob's executive camper parked in the lot. The guards approached me and said, "Hey, you can't come back here." But Bob saw me and said, "Oh, she's okay," and invited me into his trailer. He asked me if I knew how to cook, and I said, "Oh yeah, sure." He said, "Well, what can you cook?" and I told him, "Anything," which was a lie because I never cooked. I just thought I could fake it. So, he said, "Well, maybe you could cook for me and some of the crew." I said, "Oh, sure," and he asked me to come back in a couple of hours. I left and went to a bookstore and started checking out cookbooks to figure out some recipes. But when I got back, he said, "Oh no, just forget it." That's how he is— very in the moment.

Then he took me in through the backstage entrance and set me up with a seat next to Larry "Ratso" Sloman, who was writing for *Rolling Stone* magazine. We talked friendly. I really didn't have anywhere to stay and was sleeping in my car, so he and his friend George let me crash at their hotel for a few nights. Dylan was staying at a resort near Plymouth, where the band was rehearsing for two weeks. No one was supposed to know where they were staying, so I had to find out myself. It took a few days, but I finally found out and started hanging out at the hotel. They'd already started filming *Renaldo and Clara* with a Canadian film crew, and that was pretty exciting. Most of the folks working the tour, like roadies, were real assholes, but the guys on the film crew were so nice. When the tour started, some of them let me crash in their rooms and left me alone.

I pretty much followed the whole 1975 tour. I'd see Bob, and he'd say hi. Some shows, he'd let me in. Other times, the stage manager, Michael O'Hearn, would let me sew patches on his pants and do little favors to get in. It was a lot of fun.

I'd remembered that Bob said he didn't like realism when I'd given him that first painting, so I decided to do an abstract and got my boyfriend to help me paint it. It was kind of hokey, but it was Bob standing under a lamp post, playing guitar. At one of his shows in Maine, I tried to give it to him, and he hated it. He gave me this *look*. There's a certain look that Bob gives you that's like daggers going into you. You just want to cringe and melt into the floor. I know he liked the first painting, especially after seeing his reaction to the second one, and I personally don't think he kept the first one in his closet.

When they played Madison Square Garden for the Hurricane Carter benefit, there was a big party backstage. Ken Regan, who was Bob's photographer, gave me a copy of the famous picture of the entire gang shot in Montreal in front of the big Rolling Thunder backdrop. Everyone's in that picture: Bob's mother, Joan Baez, Joan's kid, Bob's kids, Sara—everyone. So, backstage at the Garden, I got everyone I could to sign it. Joni Mitchell, Roger McGuinn, Mick Ronson, and Bob all signed it. He wrote "Love, Bobby." Unfortunately, I didn't have the right kind of pen. It was a felt tip, and it faded.

Bob was funny. I was with Ratso when he signed the photo, and I think he thought that sometimes both of us could be a little annoying, hanging around all the time. So, he told me that if Ratso and I got married, he'd play at our wedding. I thought, "Man, we could get married and get divorced the next day, and it'd be fun!" But Bob probably wouldn't have shown up anyway. That first Rolling Thunder tour was such magic; there was nothing like that ever again.

In January 1976, I left Vermont and moved out to California. When they started the second Rolling Thunder tour that year, I didn't have any money and couldn't go. But then I met this guy who had $800 and an old Buick, and I said, "Hey, you want to go follow Dylan?" He said, "Sure." The tour was in Texas when we joined up. We didn't know where they were staying or even exactly where they were playing; we just knew the town. But, back then, I had this strange magic with Dylan. We were driving on the freeway near Austin when we suddenly saw his bus. It was incredible. We followed the bus to the hotel, where I connected with some of the guys and went to some of the parties.

The next town they played in, my boyfriend and I were just getting to the hotel at 3:00 A.M. when some cops pulled us over. It was 1976 in Texas and very scary. My boyfriend got really mad, because we had some weed in the car. The cops said, "What are you doing?" I said, "We're with Dylan's Rolling Thunder tour." Then they asked, "Do you have any drugs in the car?" and my boyfriend said no. The cop said, "Well, you'd better tell me if you do, because if we find some, you're going to be in trouble." So we told him the truth; we just had a quarter-ounce or something. They took the bag and dumped it out in the parking lot and said, "Okay, *go*," and didn't even give us a ticket. Things like that happened a lot when I was around Bob; there was this incredible energy that was like a shield.

I didn't see Bob much on that tour. He had his kids around and was more protected. There was no film crew, and he was more uptight than he'd been the year before. There was one show in Texas where I saw him. I can't remember what town, but the show was sold out. Tickets had been sold as reserved seating, but on the day of the show, they'd all been changed to general admission. The crowd was really upset, because they'd paid for reserved seats. I was hanging out in back by the buses, hoping I would see Bob, when he came out and called me over to ask what was going on with the crowd. I told him, and he thanked me. He didn't know anything about it and was noticeably disturbed by it.

Since we weren't connected with the tour, we didn't have access to itineraries and had to figure things out on our own. Sometimes, when the crew checked out of their hotel, they'd leave their doors open, and I'd go in and find an itinerary that told me where they were staying at the next stop on the tour. I remember getting to the hotel in Oklahoma and checking in before the buses arrived. I asked the front desk to give us a room that was *not* near the people from Rolling Thunder. What they didn't know was that, for most of the tour, the band and crew stayed in one part of the hotel and Bob stayed in another under an assumed name (Kiki Laundry, in this case).

So, they gave us a room that was supposedly on the other side but was actually right above Bob's. This was one of those hotels where the room's doors go to the outside, and I was standing outside when he came out of his room and saw me. He was blown away: "How did you get here? How did you get here?" Then he asked if I had any food in my room, but, unfortunately, I didn't. He also asked a couple of questions about my boyfriend, because he didn't know him. I assured him that he was cool. Bob was really protective because his kids were around. Eventually, we left the tour and headed to New York.

I didn't see him again until 1978, when he played the Oakland Coliseum. He was staying at the Marriott in Berkeley, so I went over to see him. I was pregnant at the time, and he was swimming in the pool when he saw me. He headed over to the hot tub and asked me to come over. I think Bob likes pregnant women. He asked if I wanted to get in the hot tub, and I told him, "Well, I don't have a bathing suit." "That's cool," he said. "You don't have to wear anything."

But I was too embarrassed; I was eight months pregnant, and it was a public pool. I ended up sitting on the edge with my feet in, and we just talked. It was so cool. If he was in a good mood, it was great. If he was in a bad mood, forget it; you didn't even go near him. But he was in a good mood, and I hadn't seen him in a couple of years. He asked what I'd been up to and was even nicer than usual. We talked for about 20 minutes, and then he got out of the hot tub and went back in the pool. When he left, I took the towel that he dried himself with.

The next time I saw him was in December 1980, when he was into the born-again thing. They were staying in San Francisco, so I went to the hotel and started hanging out in the lobby. There were a lot of people around, so Bob's management started kicking everyone out. After trying to get in for days, I finally just walked in and acted like I was staying there. I got in the elevator to go up, and who gets in the elevator with me, but Dylan. It was just me and him. He started asking how I'd been and how my grandmother was doing. Again, he asked if I had any food on me, and, again, I didn't. It was so incredible. I asked if I could take a picture of him with my daughter, who was two at the time. He told me to come back later and said he'd meet me at a certain time, but he never showed up. I went to every one of those shows. It was really easy to get in, because a lot of people weren't going for the Jesus thing. Jerry Garcia even showed up one night.

I didn't see him for a long time after that, probably six or seven years. After John Lennon was killed, it became very difficult to get to Bob. He got really paranoid, and security tightened up. He was playing the Warfield in San Francisco, and someone I knew got me backstage to see him. I could see he was a bit confused when he saw me, like he wasn't quite sure who I was. Then he said, "Oh, Olivia, you've changed your hair color." It's such an honor that he knows who I am and remembers me. I asked him to re-sign that picture of the Rolling Thunder Revue, because his autograph had faded. He did, and we just talked awhile. I gave him a charm made out of walrus tusk that I got in Alaska. It was supposed to bring good luck. He didn't really want to take it, because everyone gives him so much stuff. It just ends up in some drawer or something. But after I stressed that it was for good luck, he took it and put it in his pocket.

Then I saw him backstage at the Concord [California] Pavilion in October 1993, when he was playing with Santana. He was very sick with the flu that night, and it wasn't a good show. He said hi to me, but he wasn't in a good mood. I gave him some herbal things to put under his tongue to help make the flu go away. He was backstage talking to Wavy Gravy, and Wavy was telling him about Ben & Jerry's Ice Cream and how Bob should do a flavor for them. He was going on about how they did the Wavy Gravy flavor, and that Bob could should come up with a name. Bob seemed very interested and said he'd think about it. He was also talking to Maria Muldaur, telling her how good it was to see her. He told her that he wanted to get together with her and spend the rest of his life with her.

The last time I saw him was around his birthday in 1994, when he played the Berkeley Community Theater and the Warfield. By this time,

Olivia's gum bichromate print for Bob. The original is in striking colors.

it was virtually impossible to get to Dylan. Bob and I have a mutual friend who's known Bob since summer camp, when they were 13. I asked our friend to ask Bob if I could give him a birthday present. He did, but Dylan told him that he didn't want me going through our mutual friend. He said that if I could get to him, he'd take it.

I put a photo collage together of a young Dylan with a camera taking a picture of himself playing with all these different Dylans coming out of his head. Then I had a friend make a gum bichromate print of it, which is a special photographic process. It was really time-consuming. I wanted to give him a copy, and our friend told me, "If you can get to him, he'll take it." Well, it was pretty impossible at the time. They were staying at the Mark Hopkins Hotel in San Francisco; I hung out, but didn't see Bob. I tried to get it to him at the Warfield, but he went from the back door right into the car. He saw me, but didn't acknowledge me. I would always go outside before the last encore, so I'd be there when he came out. He'd usually go right into his bus, but the second night he played Berkeley, there was a motorcycle parked right behind the bus. He either knew the person on the bike or wanted to look at it, so he came out with this towel on his head. This big disguise, you know. Like no one would recognize him with the towel on his head. When he walked over to look at the bike, I ducked underneath the guard's arm and ran up to Bob and said, "Hey, you said you'd take this if I could get to you." I showed him the collage, and he looked at it and said, "I can't really take it right now. Give it to our friend." He plays these games. It's a hunt. You get to the finish and then the rules change. I gave it to our friend, and he gave it to Dylan. But Bob ended up giving it back to him to give to me. He said he liked it, but that it would just end up in the infamous drawer.

I still go to all the shows he plays out here, but now it's almost impossible to get to him. I don't feel that connection the way I used to. I wish I did. Back in the '70s, there was something definitely magical going on. It's too bad that it's not still like that, but when all is said and done, he's still something of a God to me.

1975

Abandoned Love

Joe Kivak

On a Thursday night in July 1975, I headed out to see Ramblin' Jack Elliott at The Bitter End in New York City. Because I wanted to learn his technique, I got there early enough to get a seat near the front so I could watch him play guitar. After the first set, a P.A. announcement told us we were welcome to stay for the second set if we honored the two-drink minimum. As the lights flashed on and I got up to leave, I glanced around the club and was stunned to see Bob Dylan seated toward the back with Jack, wearing the same striped tee shirt and leather jacket he had on in a photo with Patti Smith on the cover of the then-current *Village Voice*.

Naturally, I sat right back down. There was absolutely no way I was leaving at that point. Soon, others began to notice him, too, so Jack and Bob left their seats and went backstage. But when the engineer set up another microphone, we knew Bob was going to sit in. The electricity in the room was tangible as the club began filling up with more bodies. Finally, Jack came out and started his set. After a couple of songs, he began "With God on Our Side." After the first few lines, he turned his head toward the back of the stage and said, "Bob, you want to help me out on this?" The place went nuts as Dylan walked onstage. I can still see that shy look on his face as he nervously squinted out into the audience. He was so nervous, in fact, that he didn't notice that the capo on his guitar was crooked and buzzing badly.

Their first song was "Pretty Boy Floyd," with Bob singing harmony and his guitar buzzing right along. Then Jack started "How Long Blues." After the first verse, he looked at Bob in a way that seemed to ask him to sing a verse. Bob simply shook his head and mouthed something inaudible.

When the song finished, however, Dylan began strumming his guitar. But since it was still buzzing, he asked Jack to trade instruments with him. At that moment, everyone in the room was in a trance; it's not every day one gets to hear an impromptu Bob Dylan performance in a tiny club. After a couple of lines, we realized he was performing a new song, with each line getting even better than the last. The song was "Abandoned Love," and it *still* is the most powerful performance I've ever heard.

Ramblin' Jack started strumming along in the beginning, but he soon realized the rarity of the moment and stopped and stepped to the side. As Bob sang, the nervousness so evident earlier vanished completely. He was so moving. There he was, hitting us with new material, with everyone hanging on his every word. It was an incredible feeling to be in that small club listening to Bob Dylan perform a new song. We all felt we were watching history in the making. After he finished, he returned to his seat near the back of the club and quietly watched the rest of the show. Jack appeared so speechless and overwhelmed by Dylan's performance that he started his next song with Bob's buzzing guitar.

Later, as we began filing out into the night onto Bleecker Street, we could see Bobby Dylan through the outside windows, leaning over his table and deep in conversation with someone, the candle in front of him highlighting his face. It's a moment I'll never forget.

Jon Sievert

San Francisco, 1975.

Catfish

Hall-of-Fame pitcher **Jim "Catfish" Hunter**, *a good old boy with style, won five World Series rings in the '70s with the Oakland A's and the New York Yankees. In 1975, Hunter's first year with the Yankees, Dylan and Jacques Levy co-wrote and recorded "Catfish" while collaborating on the* Desire *LP. The song didn't make the album, but bassist/bandleader Rob Stoner frequently performed a rocking version on the Rolling Thunder Revue that year. Catfish died in September 1999 at age 53, six months after submitting this story.*

The first year I played with the New York Yankees, a guy from my hometown wrote a song called "The Catfish Kid." One day, a friend of mine said,

"Hey Catfish, there's a song out there about you, buddy."

"Yeah, I know. That guy from my hometown wrote it."

"You mean Bob Dylan's from your hometown?"

"No," I replied suspiciously. "Are you saying Bob Dylan wrote a song about me?"

That's when I found out he'd written "Catfish" and was playing it at his shows. I just couldn't believe it. I was so flattered he thought enough of me to write a song about me. He must have really been a sports fan, particularly of the New York Yankees. I know I've been a fan of his since the first time I heard him sing "Blowin' in the Wind."

1977

What Was It You Wanted?

Larry Cragg *has been a guitar technician to the stars for three decades, starting with Carlos Santana in 1970. His primary allegiance for the past 25 years has been to Neil Young, with whom he tours as a guitar technician, utility musician, and all-around assistant. He's played pedal steel guitar, banjo, baritone sax, Hammond organ, and piano onstage and in the recording studio with Young. He is the owner of Larry Cragg Guitar Repair and Vintage Instrument Rental [(415) 453-3336)] in San Anselmo, California.*

My first exposure to Bob Dylan was in concert, when I was a freshman in high school in Chicago. Our school had some kind of deal that gave us a special price for a folk music concert series at Orchestra Hall. I remember looking at the list of 10 shows and thinking, "Who's this guy Bob *Dye-lan*? I've never heard his name or his music. But, what the hell, I'll go down and see Bob *Dye-lan*." So, this guy comes onstage with an old Martin D-18 and a harmonica, and looking pretty high. I'm not normally a "words" sort of guy, but I heard the words of his songs that night—"Hard Rain's A-Gonna Fall," "The Times They Are A-Changin'," and all that stuff. I thought, "Wow, that's pretty cool," and became a fan.

The next time I saw him, I was working for him. I started fixing his guitars in 1976 or 1977, down in Los Angeles. I'm sort of a traveling guitar doctor, and they flew me in while he was finishing up an album and getting ready to tour. It was a real interesting scene down there—a bunch of bikers and all kinds of people like that. I smoked a little pot in the back room while I fixed guitars; that was normal. I went through all his guitars and asked him what gauge strings he used and how high he liked the action, because I set up guitars different for different people depending on how they play. He didn't know any of that stuff and didn't much care. He was very aloof about it all. It was kind of like working for Mike Bloomfield, who was the same way.

So, I went through everything and set him up to the best of my ability, making sure the intonation was right. I also worked on everyone else's instruments at the same time. Of course, the bass player and the other guitar players knew what they wanted. It really helps to have everybody's instruments set up by one guy so when everyone plays an *A* chord, it will really be an in-tune *A* chord.

One of the guitars I worked on was a really nice two-tone '50s [Fender] Stratocaster that Eric Clapton had just given him. While I was there, Eric

Jon Sievert

Larry Cragg in his shop in 1978. The white National guitar, dubbed "Rimbaud," was used on the Rolling Thunder Revue. Dylan can be seen playing slide on it on "Shelter From the Storm" in the video of the *Hard Rain* TV special. The guitar in the foreground is Carlos Santana's custom-built Yamaha.

called Bob and told him he'd changed his mind about giving away this great old guitar, but Dylan refused to return it. When I went to visit him a few years later, he still had it. I don't know if he eventually gave it back, but it was some sort of special guitar to Eric.

At one point, Dylan told me, "I'm through with Martin guitars. Gibsons are the ones for me. I've got three Martins I want to sell." One was that great 1960 D-28 he'd used on the Rolling Thunder Revue tour. He also had two really nice 000-18s from the '50s he wanted to get rid of. I bought the D-28, which I call Bob, for $500 and took the other two up to Prune Music in Mill Valley, where I hung them on the wall to sell. I thought it would be cool and told everyone, "Hey, those are Bob Dylan's guitars." But they just hung there for five or six months. Nobody bought them. Then I got a call from Dylan's people asking if I had any guitars that were really good for recording. I said, "Yeah, we've got a couple of really great 000-18's here, and you own them." I sent them back. Thinking back on it now, it's surprising that none of my customers made a big deal out of Dylan's guitars. Anyone could have bought them.

I can't remember exactly what year it was, probably 1979, but when I got to the rehearsal studio he'd always used, everything was different. There were a lot of people in suits hanging around, and the coffee tables had religious literature on them. I thought, "Wow, that's different," and went into the back room and started working on the guitars. But when I lit up a joint, some guy in a suit came rushing in, saying, "No, you can't do that." A year before it had been OK, but suddenly I had really screwed up. That's when he really got into the religious thing.

The last time I saw him was around 1992. Neil [Young] was doing a solo acoustic tour and playing an extended run at some New York theater. Bob showed up backstage every night. No one recognized him because he was wearing a hooded sweatshirt and looked like a homeless guy. So, he asks me if he can have one of Neil's harmonica holders. Here's the guy who made these things popular in the first place, but there were only three of this particular kind left on the planet, and they were all wired up with special wireless hardware. I just couldn't give him one. After I told him that, he didn't like me much. And he honestly didn't recognize me, either, though I'd worked on his guitars for five years. Elliot Roberts [Young's manager] introduced me, and I could see a blank stare.

1977

Jokerman

Joel Stein, *48, is an attorney who lives in the metropolitan Boston area. At age 16, he heard "Like a Rolling Stone" and was hooked. "I didn't really understand the words," he says, "but I loved the attitude and have followed his career closely since then."*

I grew up in Queens and attended New York University from 1969 to 1973. Dylan was a hero to the NYU population, and we would regularly pass in front of his house on MacDougal Street and shout, "Hey Bob, can you please crawl out your window?"

In 1977, a couple of years after graduation, I was back in Greenwich Village visiting a friend and having dinner at a club called The Other End. As we talked, I noticed my friend staring behind me and subtly pointing for me to turn around. When I did, I saw Bob Dylan standing behind me with a couple of his friends.

Dylan, Bob Neuwirth, and several others sat down at the table right next to us. Mike Porco, the club's owner, immediately joined them. I was now faced with one of life's major decisions. Do I say anything to Dylan or not? Finally, after mustering up the courage and discussing with my friend what would be a "cool" thing to say, I felt ready to go.

I walked up to Dylan's table, looked him directly in the eyes, and said, "Hey, aren't you one of the Supremes?"

Bob Neuwirth laughed, several of the other people seated smiled, and Dylan glared. After several long moments of silence, he looked directly at me and said with a raised voice, *"No, I'm not."*

Stunned, I slithered back to my table in shame, ordered a few more drinks, and attempted to enjoy the rest of my evening.

1977

As I Went Out One Morning

Dave Whiting-Smith, *38, is a guitarist, painter, and poet who works as a chef's assistant in Paso Robles, California. He's been a Dylan fan since seeing the* Hard Rain *television special in 1976. "He's my favorite artist, bar none. I don't judge Dylan; I just love him and most of what he does." Dave's e-mail address is* starcruzer40@yahoo.com.

In Spring of '77, two friends and I went to Point Dume to hang around Bob's Bluewater Street home, the one with the copper dome. Before leaving on our little trip, we picked up a shopping bag of high-grade weed from our secret "dope tree" in Reseda.

We get to Bob's and proceed to throw a Frisbee around 'till I get bored and toss it in his front yard. His gate guard comes slowly strolling out with some medieval torture device and a coupla black Labs. Before he can say anything, I say, "Wanna bong?," and he says, "Do I wanna ball?" And I say, "No, ya wanna bong?" He says, "Do I wanna ball you?" I say, "No, *bong*. Ya know, *smoke*." He says, "Well, *okay*. We show him our stash, and he invites us in. We're shitting bricks as we walk down Dylan's dirt driveway, which is lined with old station wagons and a couple hearses.

We go into a little guard shack that has a two chairs, a heater, and a fridge that's full, top to bottom, with Budweiser. He told us Bob was home, and I asked if, perhaps, he could invite him out for a smoke. While we were standing there, various Hollywood-type characters were showing up and getting the okay from the house to come in. The guard didn't wanna talk about Bob, though he got very hostile when I asked him how much Bob paid. He yelled, "Not enough!" and kicked the wall for emphasis.

Then Dylan's gardener showed up, a very nice surfer-type dude, but intelligent. He said Bob's screening device for people he doesn't know is the front half of a '65 Mustang built into the base of the house. It has a reverse periscope thing that allows Bob to watch you sitting behind the wheel before letting you in. He also said the living room floor was just beach sand.

The gardener said he played hoops with Bob when he was around. When I asked about visitors like myself, he said that Joan of Arc had been there just the week before, and that Jesus and Buddha were recent gate-crashers as well. He said Bob is quiet and a very nice guy to work for, but that he's very sneaky and comes and goes without being noticed fairly often.

Well, the day wore on, and as the sun began to set, we left, sad that Bob didn't come out, but quite thrilled just to have spent a day on his property, knowing he was right around the corner.

1978

Wanted Man

Timothy Chisholm *was born and raised in a Chicago suburb and currently teaches at a middle school in Southern California. He can be contacted at* tchiz@snowline.net.

It's not a story I tell often. Like describing a secret handshake to the uninitiated, I feared cheapening the experience by retelling it to those unable to comprehend its significance. It's been a secret treasure in my trunk of memories for 20 years. I expect that anyone who purchases this book, or even takes the time to browse through it, is probably interested enough to appreciate the value this story holds for me. It's all true, and until now, it's been all mine.

Saturday, October 28, 1978. I was a student at Southern Illinois University in Carbondale. Halloween was being celebrated in an outrageously wild fashion of long-standing tradition. It was also Homecoming, which added to the festive atmosphere. It was Mardi Gras in the Midwest, and the town was overflowing with costume-clad revelers. It was the day Bob Dylan came to town.

It seemed everyone I'd known since kindergarten was there. Some I hadn't seen in 10 years. They were there to party, but they were also hoping to get a ticket to that night's concert. I had camped out in front of the arena box office for three nights before tickets went on sale. I still wound up with 20th-row seats, but was grateful to at least be on the main floor. Later, I discovered that a good friend worked at the box office. Unbeknownst to me, she'd managed to secure two tickets, front-row center. I'd been a renowned Dylan fan for years, and Julie was genuinely pleased to give those tickets to me. I'm sure she knew no one who'd appreciate them more.

So, when Dylan took the Carbondale stage, a stop on his *Street Legal* tour, I was there at the foot of the altar with my high school chum Dave Dewey. The moment Dylan hit the stage, I was on my feet. I stood on my chair the entire show, dancing, cheering, singing every word. I played imaginary guitar and contributed my own percussion. Friends seated way in back told me later that they'd spent as much time watching my performance as they did Dylan's. If I had known, or been in any condition to think logically about it, I probably would have toned it down a bit. I was simply in my own world, transported by music and lyrics I knew so well, and which meant so much. Except for a brief glance at the audience around me, wondering how they could possibly remain seated at a time like this, I didn't notice anyone but Bob Dylan. Apparently, Dylan noticed me as well.

He finished his first set with a scorching harmonica solo to close "It's All Over Now Baby Blue." Then, in slow motion, Dylan stepped to the edge of the stage and tossed his harmonica to me. I was completely unprepared. I actually caught it in self-defense; otherwise it would have hit me smack in the face. Immediately, a surge of fans leaping for the sacred artifact crushed me. I was on the floor, buried beneath a pile of hopeful lunatics. My friend Dave pulled the disappointed mob off and then stared at me. At first, I thought that he was concerned for my physical well-being, but no, he was just fascinated by that darned harmonica. He reverently asked if he could see and touch it. Not wanting to seem possessive or greedy, I handed it over for his inspection. I was concerned for its safety and wondered about its whereabouts for a bit, but soon I was back in the music, completely oblivious.

The rest of the concert flew by. The band was tight, and the music

The author's front-row ticket and gift from Bob Dylan.

was red hot. But it was at the end of the concert, when Dylan and his band returned for an encore, that events turned toward a most memorable meeting. Dave and I were pressed against the edge of the stage, and we agreed that this screaming was ridiculous. We were giddy, even hysterical with laughter. We knew Dylan couldn't really see or hear anyone. He was squinting into the lights, and the noise was deafening. Dave and I decided to have a good time shouting along with the crowd. We began screaming ridiculous lines at Bob from 10 feet away. It was a joke; we thought we were making fun of the "Dylanmania" around us. So, as Dylan and his band launched into a rousing encore of "Changing of the Guards," I began shouting,

"Hey Bob! Look at me, man. C'mon, Bob, you can look at me."

Dave thought that was funny, and it spurred him to push the limits of hilarity. He began shouting, "Hey Dylan, fuck you, man."

That cracked us both up. After all, he couldn't hear us. I'm sure the fans around us thought we were insane, but that just made things even more hysterically funny to us. When the song ended, Dylan waved to the crowd and was gone. Dave and I, along with some other friends who'd made their way to the front, hung around until the house lights went up and it was obvious Dylan wasn't coming back. We headed for the exit.

I made it to the lobby and was heading out the door, when someone I knew stopped me and said there was a man back inside looking for me. I didn't question it; perhaps I'd lost my wallet and someone was trying to return it. It didn't occur to me that I hadn't brought a wallet that night. I was floating, unquestioning, and made my way back inside.

There was a small crowd gathered in front of the stage, everyone looking wide-eyed as I approached. A young man behind the security partition pointed at me and told me to follow him. He handed me a pass and led me to a gate. I was thinking maybe the roadies were looking to invite a few folks to a post-concert party, for local color, you know? But as he opened the gate, I realized that he wanted me to follow him backstage.

Suddenly, I was nervous. What was all this about? Everyone was staring at me, slack-jawed. Right then, I spotted an old high school friend, Kevin McGugan, who was in town for the festivities. During the concert, he was seated well in back, but he was here now. I grabbed his arm and said, "He's coming with me." Kevin was handed his own backstage pass, and we followed our guide, who never said another word. He signaled us to wait, then disappeared down a long corridor, at the end of which was the men's locker room. (The SIU Arena is where the basketball team frequently holds court.)

I was uneasy, scared even, but Kevin was looking around like a kid at Disneyland. I don't know why I was so apprehensive. I just knew something important was happening and said to Kevin, "Stick by me, man." He understood and spoke the only words he uttered the whole time we were backstage: "Don't worry, Chiz. I won't let anything happen to you."

Our guide stepped out of the locker room and motioned to us. A handful of people were loitering outside the locker room door, and as we approached, I heard someone say, "Oooooh, a command performance." I still didn't get it. I should have known what was coming, but my mind couldn't wrap itself around the idea that Bob Dylan had requested to meet me. I truly had no idea, even as Kevin and I stepped into his dressing room.

He was standing there with his shirt off, and it was obvious he'd just washed the stage makeup off his face. I was struck by how remarkably wide he was. I mean, he was lean, not an extra ounce on him, but his shoulders, they were so...well, wide.

My mind started racing a mile a minute, trying to make sense of this situation. There was Bob Dylan standing directly in front of me. A thought flashed through my brain. It was like one of those last requests granted by the Make-A-Wish Foundation. Maybe that was it. I must be dying of some insidious blood disease or a brain tumor, and only my mom knows. So, she set up this meeting between her beloved son and his idol. The thought was gone in an instant. I stepped forward as Dylan held out his hand. As we shook, I asked, "Why are you doing this?"

"You really added to the show tonight," he said.

I started to tell him how fantastic the concert was, how much I loved it, when Dylan spoke again, "I don't know what your one friend's problem was, though."

In retrospect, it was obvious he was talking about Dave and his shouting of "Fuck you, Bob!" while laughing hysterically. An hour later, I figured out what Dylan was referring to. But at that moment, I honestly couldn't guess what he was talking about.

"Who?" I asked. "The guy on my right? That would be your left."

"No," Bob said. "The guy on your left. Would be my right."

I tried to picture it, but eventually shook my head in confusion. I looked to Kevin for help, but he was just watching the scene with a transcendent grin. Thankfully, Dylan let it go.

I told Bob how much I enjoyed the new versions of his old songs. I wanted to thank him for the harmonica, but I didn't know where it was at the time. Dave told me when the show was over that he'd lost it. I knew he was probably just screwing with my mind; he *had* to have it. (He did, I found out later.) But I wasn't positive, so I didn't mention the harmonica. I was incredibly cool. I didn't act like a hysterical schoolgirl. I didn't ask for an autograph. I didn't question him about the meaning of obscure lyrics. Hell, I even had a camera under my jacket, but I had no intention of asking him to pose for a picture. This was a notoriously private man, and I didn't want to do anything to threaten the perfect moment.

Then Dylan asked, "So, is there anything you want, anything I can give you?" As he said his, he gestured casually toward the food laid out across the table. I wasn't sure if Dylan was inviting us to eat something or what, so I replied, "Oh, no thanks, man. You've already done more than enough."

I was thinking that what I'd really like to do is go have a beer with him and hang out together. Let him get to know me...become friends. Instead I said, "There's not really time for what I'd like."

It was a strange thing to say, but Dylan nodded his head in understanding. We both looked at the floor, and then came the moment I treasure the most—shared silence. He wasn't trying to get rid of us. There was no anxious need to fill the silence with pointless conversation. We simply stood together. Dylan tapped his toe, not with impatience, but in time to the music playing in his head. Then we looked at one another. Dylan again nodded his head, I nodded back.

At that point, reality came rushing back in. I knew there were dozens of people outside who would never believe this. I needed some concrete proof, so I said, "Well, Bob, since you asked, how about some tickets for tomorrow night's show?"

"Yeah?" he says, "Where is it?" This elicits a giggle from Kevin.

"St. Louis," I answered.

"How far is that from here?"

Kevin and I both laughed at the idea that he didn't know where he was or where he was going.

"Oh, it's a couple of hours away."

"You'd go that far to see me?" he asked incredulously.

"Are you kidding?" I shot back. "That's nothing. We drove 12 hours round trip to see you in Chicago." Bob Dylan looked impressed.

"Sure, okay" he said. "Just ask the guy outside the door; he'll take care of it."

And that was our cue. I thanked him for everything, and as we headed out the door, I called over my shoulder, "May God bless you, man."

Back in the corridor, we were greeted by questioning stares from the group outside the dressing room. "He told us to ask someone out here about tickets for tomorrow night," I shouted.

A fellow stepped up with a small notepad in his hand. "How many you need?"

Boy, that's a good question, I thought to myself. Everyone I knew was in town, and I was certain they'd all like a ticket. Then again, I didn't want to overdo it.

"Uh, six," I said.

"Six? Why not just ask for six dozen?" he replied, his voice rising.

I'd seen *Don't Look Back* a few times, so I was aware of the tendency for mind games by those in Dylan's inner circle. Was this guy one of them? Was he trying to give me hell? Well, I was unflappable. That night I was positively bulletproof.

"Hey, Bob said to talk to someone out here about tickets," I said. "But if it's going to be a problem, then just forget the whole thing."

I turned on my heel and began walking down the corridor. Everyone was caught completely off guard, even Kevin, who scurried to catch up. It took a few moments, but the fellow with the notepad chased after us.

"Hey, okay, okay...six tickets. What's your name?"

"Chisholm."

"Okay." He wrote it in his notepad.

"So, what's the deal? Are there gonna be tickets or what?" I asked.

"Yeah, yeah...at the box office."

And he wasn't lying. Six tickets were waiting under my name at the box office in St. Louis the next night. Another great show, although I'd lost my voice by then and was running on two days without sleep. In fact, I was in a fog for at least two weeks after meeting Bob Dylan. I skipped a lot of classes and spent a lot of time grinning and reliving that once-in-a-lifetime experience. I found it extraordinary that such a private man would reach out and connect in such a personal way.

Twenty years later, Bob Dylan won a Grammy for his album *Time Out Of Mind*. In his acceptance speech, he told a story of being 16 or 17 years old and seeing Buddy Holly at the Duluth National Armory.

"I was three feet away," Dylan said, "and he looked at me."

Yeah, I know just how that feels.

1985

Honey, Just Allow Me One More Chance

Veronica Lambert *lives in Spain and is a primary school teacher and psychologist-turned-translator, from Catalan and Spanish into English. Introduced to Dylan's music at age 20 through* Blonde on Blonde, *she now owns all of his albums "and a fairly decent collection of outtakes and concerts." Her web site is located at* http://members.xoom.com/veronica_m_l/home.htm.

July 1st was a warm afternoon in Catalonia, Spain. I drove a group of friends to Barcelona to see Bob Dylan, my all-time hero, perform that night. The *Poble Espanyol* is sort of a mini-town made up of small replicas of famous Spanish buildings and squares. It's a beautiful setting for concerts, which are held on an end stage in the main square.

We arrived with plenty of time to spare, so my friends decided to have a look around the arena. I had other plans; I wanted to search the area and find the most likely place for Bob to come off stage. I spent ages looking before I decided I'd found the place. There were several exits from the stage area, but all but one would take Bob into very crowded parts of the square. It seemed likely that would probably be the one he'd use.

I waited in vain at that spot for what seemed like ages to see if he'd appear. When I heard the band cranking up, signaling the start of the concert, I rushed around to the front to see the show. Of course, it was fabulous. When the encores began, I excused myself from my friends and returned to "my spot." When I asked one of the bodyguards where Bob would come off stage, he pointed to another exit. As I was making my way there, something intuitively told me it wasn't the right one, so I returned to my original spot.

Minutes later, just after the show ended, I saw Bob walking alone down the back steps of the stage. As he came closer to where I stood, I called out to him.

"*Bobby.*"

He looked my way, and, to my great joy and disbelief, walked right over. I was dumbstruck, which is unusual for me.

"Hi there," he said.

I told him I loved the show, and we talked about a few of the songs he'd performed. He asked me which ones I'd enjoyed the most. A few people who were obviously with his organization walked up to where we stood, clearly expecting Bob to go with them. I was just standing there looking into his beautiful blue eyes when he took hold of my hands and held them for a few seconds before saying good-bye. I remember his hands felt as cold as ice. All I could think to say was, "I love you, Bob." It's a bit embarrassing when I think back on it now.

My impression was that he was a very genuine person, the same as you or me, and not the disagreeable jerk he's sometimes made out to be by the press. After sharing my adventure with my friends, they thought I was totally crazy. But that didn't concern me. I went home on Cloud Nine that night. I felt that I could die happily at any point, now that I had met my idol.

Two years later, on July 24, 1985, Dylan returned to the *Poble Espanyol.* I decided to go to the concert on my own this time and get there early. I must admit feelings of nervousness raced through me. Half of me thought that if I'd got the chance meet him once, then I could do it again. The other half was nagging that I wouldn't be so lucky this time and would wind up feeling disappointed.

I arrived at the venue while the equipment was still being set up, only to discover that the band was about to do a sound check and everyone in the surrounding area would have to leave the square immediately. I tried to hide in some shrubbery, but I was caught and ordered to leave the area at once. The place was teeming with bodyguards; not just a few local lads as on the previous occasion, but a group of big guys from America armed with walkie-talkies.

I missed catching Bob at the beginning of the concert, but as the encores started, I again strolled over to the spot where I'd first encountered him. The show ended...no Bob. Rumor had it he'd left by another exit, and I decided to wait around to see for myself. A half-hour dragged by as plates of food went in and out of the stage area. The bodyguards kept urging me to go home, but I told them in no uncertain terms that I had a letter and a small gift I wanted to give Bob. They laughed, saying there was no way I'd ever get close enough to Dylan to give him anything. Besides, they sneered, he didn't accept gifts from fans. I informed them I was still going to hang around and see for myself.

Eventually, my patience paid off. The bodyguards suddenly started talking like mad into their walkie-talkies. One of them sent two others to watch over me, assuming I was going to be trouble.

Bob finally emerged dressed in jeans and a checked shirt. To my dismay, he was immediately circled by about eight guards, and they all began marching toward the gate.

Once again, I called out, "*Bobby*," and once again he looked my way. I couldn't believe it as he began walking toward me, just as he had two years before. My legs felt like they were going to give out.

When he approached me, I said, "Bob, I have a letter and a gift for you. Will you accept them?" His bright blue eyes bore right into mine. "Yes, I will," he said. "Thanks a lot, honey."

As he reached out to take them from me, the bodyguards who'd been sent to keep an eye on me stepped in and tried to block me from giving the items to Bob. Good old Bob just shoved them away and held out his hand to accept them, which annoyed the guards incredibly.

Once again, Bob Dylan held my hand for a few seconds, and I was able to stroke the softness of his skin and gaze into those amazingly intense eyes. I felt such empathy for him at that moment. He looked so tired and lonely—a prisoner of his own fame, a bird trapped in a cage.

I feel so privileged to have met Bob Dylan not once, but twice. I'm just sorry that I'll probably never get to know him. I imagine he must be a very special person to have as a friend.

1985

New York Driven Women #12 & 35

Gary Pig Gold, *44, is a guitarist, singer, producer, and promoter based in Hoboken, New Jersey. He is also the editor of* The Pig Paper, *Canada's first punk fanzine, which he founded in 1975.*

B ob's ex-wife Sara sits on the bleachers in a smoky little Hoboken nightclub watching her latest son-in-law belt out his latest demo tape to an appreciative, but small, audience of friends and scene-schemers. Bob's ex-wife certainly looks beautiful despite her too many years of lawsuits and sleepless nights. She's still slim and dark, and her eyes still sparkle mischievously with the magic of eras gone by.

"I'm here tonight, really, to support him," she tells me, as she glances supportively at the figure anxiously replacing a string in mid-verse. "Of course, I know only too well how much it takes to step out on that stage with only a song between you and...," her hand sweeps over the dance

110

floor, "them. It's a tough game. No, wait a minute...it isn't a game. It's a way of life, isn't it? It is life for them, isn't it? All these singers, all these kids, all their songs. But what can it really all add up to? In the end I mean?"

Strange to hear Bob Dylan's ex-wife unloading baggage onto a stranger like me—and in Hoboken. But then, one doesn't get to be Bob's ex by keeping one's thoughts to oneself, I should imagine.

"You'll excuse me now, won't you?" she smiles as a final chord fades from the speakers. "I must get Peter out of his wet shirt and into a dry cab." Bob's ex-wife pops to her feet, and with a somehow sincere "Take care" flung at me over a shoulder, she rushes around the nearest corner out of view.

Bob's ex-girlfriend called me at 11:30 one night. She wondered if I could possibly make it over to help her arrange some songs. "I have a show Monday night, and I'm absolutely frantic," she bleated. "It'll only take an hour or so. I promise."

Ten minutes later, I'm deposited outside her building on one of the Upper East Side's most uppity blocks. I look up to see her already waving crazily through her Pella windows. A second later, she's dashed downstairs to haul me in.

"I'm sorry, I'm really sorry, but the intercom's on the blink and we're between doormen. And during this, of all weeks. I'm really terribly sorry, but you know what they say about if it's not one thing, it's another." I'm scrambling to keep apace as she whisks me through the lobby and up the stairs to her majestic double-oak doors. Bob's ex-girlfriend's apartment is huge and sumptuous in the extreme, despite the fact that its lone contents at the moment are a futon, a piano, and a fireplace full of orchids. "I'm sorry there's nowhere to sit yet—there's hardly anything to eat yet—but I've only just moved in three nights ago, and my furniture's still somewhere between here and the coast. At least I hope it is. With the kind of week I've been having, I'll bet the trucks have broken down somewhere in the wilds of Minnesota, and I'll be living on Ritz Bits for the rest of my life."

As I glance overhead at the ornate chandelier and, higher still, clumps of Renaissance angels painstakingly painted on the ceilings, I can't help but realize a large percentage of Grand Central Station's homeless could spend their remaining days comfortably in Bob's ex-girlfriend's closet.

"Okay, okay. I have half an hour, maybe 45 minutes to do on Monday. And between the fittings and the pre-shoot, what am I going to do about this hair? I have to whittle down the absolute best set of songs I can before I hire all the backup people. I think it's important above all else to show-case the width and the depth of my repertoire. After all, we're no spring chickens here. I mean, I've been working the Village since I was 14.

"I met Bob back in '65, you know. What a little twerp he was then. Sometimes, I still call him my little twerp. Anyway, I met him in one of those awful dessert places on Bleeker, and Bobby was, how shall I put this...shit-faced. He was drunk, okay? And he was hitting on me, for God's sake. Hitting on me. And I just kept saying to him, 'Get away from me you little twerp,' but he could not leave me alone. All night he's going, 'You're beautiful. What's your name?' And I was so young and so scared, I just wanted to get out of there. But Bobby said, and I'll never forget this, 'That's okay. That's okay. We're gonna meet again someday, out on the coast.' And damn it, nine years, and just about as many husbands, later I'm out in L.A., searching everywhere for the man. And would you believe it? We met again just like he said. And you know what? He's just as big a little twerp today as he ever was."

By 4:00 A.M. I was getting hungry and even a little bit tired. Not that I mind listening to Bobspeak upon Bobspeak direct from the ex-girl-friend's mouth, as it were.

"I'm awfully sorry. I don't want to keep you all night, but would you believe I don't even have a clock here? With my luck, I've left it out on the coast, not that you ever need to know the time out there. But thank you so very much for coming by so late on such short notice. You know I appreciate it very much. But I'm sorry, I've got these damn fittings and that damn check thing of mine all day tomorrow, and, God, will I ever get everything banged together by Monday night?"

Bob Dylan's ex-girlfriend saw me into another cab, and, you know, we never did get to work on any songs.

Street Rock

Hip-hop pioneer **Kurtis Blow** *brought rap from the street to the record-buying masses with his funky 1980 dance classic, "The Breaks," rap's first certified gold record. His production work for other artists has netted critical praise and a host of awards. Currently living in Los Angeles, he's just started his own record label, Groove Records, and will release his 25th Anniversary album in 2000. Among his professional accomplishments, Kurtis recruited Dylan to rap on "Street Rock," the opening cut on his 1986 Mercury LP,* Kingdom Blow.

I first met Bob in 1983, when were recording at the Power Station on 57th Street and 11th Avenue in New York. It was a big, hot, mega-studio that charged $250 an hour when $250 an hour was unheard of. Many of the big rock-and-roll stars recorded there. I was in one room recording some backup singers for an album, and Dylan was in the adjacent room. He heard my singers and asked if he could use them. I knew from studying music in school that he was a folklore hero and legend. His lyrics in the '60s helped with the civil rights movement. I lent him my singers.

When I was making *Kingdom Blow*, I thought, "Wow, I know Bob Dylan. I'm going to ask him for a favor. He borrowed my singers, maybe he'll do a rap for me." I had heard he was a rapper, and a lot of his songs seemed like rap music to me. I had "Street Rock," which had an intro that was four bars or eight bars, and I asked him to do it. He said, "Sure. I remember you, Kurtis," and invited me and my road manager to fly out to California. We got a limo and drove out to his Malibu studio with my 24-track tape.

My road manager, Wayne Valentine, is a huge, 6' 2", 350-pound black guy, but soft as a puppy inside. He can look threatening, but his smile and demeanor usually suggest otherwise. While driving up the winding hills to Dylan's house, I remember Bob's warning: "I've got this big Great Dane out here, but he's a wonderful dog. Don't worry, he doesn't bite people." And Wayne was saying, "Kurtis, man, I don't like dogs." I was like, "Oh, man, don't worry about it."

We get there, ring the buzzer, and push through two-way doors leading to the studio. Actually, he's got two or three studios, and we had to walk down this long hall to get to the one where Bob was. Suddenly, the Great Dane runs out, barking up a storm. He jumps at Wayne and growls, and Wayne starts running at top speed down the hall, bursting through those two-way doors...*boom*. It was so funny to see this huge guy running down the hall away from the dog. Bob and I laughed and laughed. Finally, Dylan went out, got the dog, and put him up. Wayne came back, and Dylan invited us into the studio.

We played him the song, and I told him what part I wanted him to do. He went right into the studio by himself, learned the lyrics, and knocked it out in one take. I was shocked and amazed. I've written raps for Sheila E, The Fat Boys, all kinds of entertainers that don't really rap. I write the raps, they go home and practice, and then come back to try it. It usually takes them several hours to get it done. This guy wrote the rap down, went into the studio, and knocked it out in one perfect take. I was thinking, "Bob, you don't even have to think about doing that one again— it's great." I was floored. It was like, okay, that's it. Time to go home. We were there maybe half an hour. He's a great guy. So cool. He's to himself a lot, quiet, doesn't talk that much. But when he does, his voice is very humble and calm.

After the record came out, I got really busy and forgot to send him a copy. His management finally called and said, "You could have had the decency to at least send Bob an album. He's pretty angry." I was so upset at myself. Dylan did the song for free...never charged me anything. A legend like Bob could have easily gotten $50,000 for participating on an album like that. So, I got the album and took it to one of his concerts at Madison Square Garden in late 1986 or early 1987. I gave it to him backstage after the show, and he was very happy to get it. He didn't seem upset with me anymore, so that was a good thing. I'm honored to have had him record on my album.

By using Dylan, I was trying to make "Street Rock" a big cross-over pop hit, but the label I was on at the time wouldn't allow it. They had policies against R&B artists crossing over into pop. Run-D.M.C. actually did it just a couple of months later when they recorded that song with Aerosmith ["Walk This Way"]. But I'd sure love to do something with Bob again. Maybe redo one of his songs...like keep the chorus but do raps. I think it would be great for both of us. Give me a call if you're reading this, Bob.

1986

Shakespeare in the Alley

Paul Guerra, *36, is an Information Systems Analyst and Y2K Coordinator who lives in Glastonbury, Connecticut.*

On a beautiful July afternoon in 1986, my brother, cousin, and I were drinking at the now-defunct Irish watering hole Sean Patrick's in downtown Hartford, Connecticut. We were getting "primed" for that night's "True Confessions" concert at the Civic Center, featuring Tom Petty and the Heartbreakers and our hero, Bob Dylan.

We finished our last round of drinks and split. As we began walking down a back alleyway on our way to the concert, we noticed two men approaching in the distance. One was carrying a guitar case, while the other shuffled along beside him.

Sarcastically, my cousin cracked, "Hey guys, maybe it's Bob Dylan."

We all chuckled...very funny. But as we got closer, we got a clearer

116

look and immediately recognized them. Howie Epstein, Petty's bass player, was carrying the guitar case, and Bob Dylan was walking beside him. We almost had heart attacks.

Crossing paths in the narrow alleyway, we just couldn't miss each other...couldn't not say something. So, just to acknowledge them, I said, "Hey there, fellows. I'm going to the show tonight."

Without hesitation, Dylan shot back, "Oh yeah? Well, isn't that a coincidence? So am I."

As soon as he said it, Howie Epstein cracked up laughing, and Bob was grinning as they strode off down the alley to the gig.

It was great enough just to encounter Dylan, but I'll never forget actually exchanging words with him and getting that wonderful smart-assed comeback.

"Bob Dylan has made a major impact on humanity, hitting the nerves of issues such as civil rights, justice for all, and awareness of our inner selves. I've particularly appreciated his spiritual songs, such as "Gotta Serve Somebody" and "In the Garden." In my mind, he's always been a poet, hitchiking down the highways of life armed with only a guitar. But this poet isn't on the road to oblivion; this poet stops to sing and share his dreams with us. God bless Bob Dylan."

—Maya Angelou

1987

It's All Over Now, Baby Blue

John Crawford

One evening in the spring of 1987, I was on duty driving my cab around Manhattan. Around 8:30, I picked up a woman about 70, who asked me to drop her off at 5th Avenue and 13th Street. We reached her destination and I turned around to tell her how much she owed. As she began digging in her purse, I casually turned back around and saw Bob Dylan standing directly in front of my cab.

For a second, I thought I was hallucinating, maybe from a lack of sleep and too much caffeine. But I quickly realized that this was real; it was him. I started waving frantically, signaling that I'd pick him up as soon as this lady finished paying, He gestured back, indicating he saw me and planned to take my cab. My legs began shaking, and my heart was racing about 100 beats a minute.

At this point, I'm completely focused on Dylan while trying to talk to the woman and remain polite. She said, "I'm looking for my money. It's in here somewhere."

I was getting anxious and said, "Ma'am, it's all right. You don't have to pay. If you just leave the cab, it's okay."

Unfortunately, that was the wrong thing to say. She became confused and said, "What? What do you mean?"

I told her straight out, "Ma'am, Bob Dylan is standing right in front of this cab, and I would really like to have him as a passenger."

"Bob who? . . . Bob who?"

I was trying to stay as cool as possible and again tried to explain the situation. Finally, she handed me the money, but it wasn't over yet. She began looking around in her pocketbook again. I was getting irritated and asked, "What are you doing back there?"

"I'm looking for more money, so I can give you a tip."

That was it. I lost my cool: "Ma'am, please. I don't want a tip."

To which she replied, "No, I always tip my cab drivers."

By now I could tell Dylan was getting a little antsy, so I waved at him to climb in. But he didn't signal back. He just kept looking right at me. Apparently, he was waiting for her to climb out.

I handed the woman back the five dollars she had just given me and said, "If you'll get out of the cab, you not only don't have to tip me, but this is yours." She went into a dialogue about how it "just didn't seem right for me not to charge her."

I looked at her and said, "Ma'am, the biggest event in my entire life would be for me to have Bob Dylan ride in my cab. Please get out."

Finally, she took back her five dollars, opened the door, and began to climb out. I looked back at Dylan and beeped my horn, waving frantically. Just then another cab pulled up behind me, and all I could do was sit there and watch as Dylan put his arm up and hailed it. Talk about disappointment. I really couldn't blame him, though, because he'd been waiting for almost five minutes, although it seemed closer to 30 to me. After all that, the woman ended up leaving a quarter tip. I'll never forget that—a 25-cent tip.

There have been only a few times in my life when I've really lost my temper. But when she got out after that "tip," as I watched Bob Dylan speed off in another cab, I was full of rage for about two minutes. I sat parked in my cab until I managed to calm down, then headed uptown back to the grind.

It's been 12 years since that day, and I'm still driving a cab in New York City. Who knows? Maybe someday I'll again see Bobby Dylan trying to hail a cab. You can bet I'll be ready this time.

1989

Drifter's Escape

Julie Woodbridge

On Monday evening, July 3, 1989, just days before my 17th birthday, Bob Dylan played Summerfest in Milwaukee. Earlier that year I had experienced my emotional "coming of age," which I largely attribute to listening to his music, and I just *knew* it was going to be a fantastic evening.

Dylan's set contained a mixture of well-known and obscure songs. But even some of the well-known pieces were almost unrecognizable at first, because of way he sang them—faster, and combining one verse with half of the next. And his vocals didn't always follow the tempo. It was almost as though he was rushing through the set, pausing but a few seconds between songs, and not uttering a word to his screaming fans. A sole spotlight illuminated him on the darkened stage. From where I sat, he was a slight, barely recognizable figure. After his last song, he walked off the stage, and the lights came on amidst our cries for an encore.

Immediately after the show, we met with friends and headed for another stage, where Johnny Winter was scheduled to perform. By the time we arrived, Winter was halfway through his first set, so we were relegated to the outer edges of the crowd of about 200. Someone to my right bumped into me, and I looked over and saw a tall guy with long, flowing blonde hair and a full beard let out a cry of "Yee haw!" As I turned back to look at the stage, I caught sight of a figure wearing Ray-Bans and a gray sweatshirt with the hood turned up. Blood rushed through my veins, as I turned to my sister Mary and pointed to the figure, now nearly obscured by the crowd. She looked at me, confused, as I screamed, *"That's Bob Dylan."*

She could barely hear me over the wailing guitar and the cries of the people, but I kept pointing. Mary glanced to her left, then back at me, shaking her head in confusion. I looked over at our friend Jim, who was staring at me as though I was crazy. He, too, had seen me pointing and screaming, and his reaction was identical to that of my sister's—total confusion, with a touch of impatience. I took their glares to mean I was mistaken. Maybe I had just been fooled by an impostor who bore a striking resemblance to Dylan, wearing a disguise to fool the crowd and attract attention. I was disgusted with myself that I, of all the people around me, was the only one who fell for it, and I turned back to the show.

But the image of the "impostor" continued to haunt me. Who the hell *else* looks like Bob Dylan? As another surge of energy flowed through me, I turned back to plead my case again, only to find my sister staring slack-jawed and Jim's eyes bulging with astonishment. Through a parting in the crowd, we saw the man in disguise again, standing only ten feet away. This time there was no doubt; we looked at each other and quickly moved as close as we could without crowding him.

Two pillars of unassuming bodyguards flanked Dylan, each with wires coming from under their polo shirts and disappearing into ear plugs. Just then, a drunk, gangly, dark-haired woman approached Dylan and screamed, "Are you Bob Dylan? Oh my God. Are you Bob Dylan?" He looked around uncomfortably, then nodded in the affirmative, and the woman tore off screeching. The bodyguards tensed up a bit, but, luckily, she attracted little attention. Those who observed the incident from the sidelines just gave acknowledging looks, smiled, and turned back to enjoy Winter's show.

Suddenly, the obnoxious woman was back, carrying a pen and what looked like a folded up receipt. "Can I have your autograph?" she trilled, thrusting the paper at him. Dylan looked left and right, not responding. "*Here*," she said in a demanding voice, shoving the paper toward him. Dylan shook his head no and took a step back. One of the bodyguards stepped forward, towering over her, and said, "*No*, you cannot talk to him; you cannot get his autograph. Please step away *now*." The lady glowered at the bodyguard and wandered off.

Presented with a once-in-a-lifetime opportunity, we tried to think of something to say to Dylan that he hadn't heard a million times before. I really love your music? You're the greatest? No, too trite, even if it is the truth. It seemed more natural and respectful to leave him alone to enjoy the music. But Jim, the free spirit among us, tapped his hand lightly on Bob's shoulder. Startled, Dylan turned around. "I just want to tell you that you sang 'John Brown' really well tonight," Jim said. "Thank you," Dylan replied, nodding and turning back to the musicians onstage.

With the help of crazy crowd logic, I found myself standing right next to him, blocked only by an occasional maneuver of his bodyguard or a Johnny Winter fan trying to get a better view. Through a series of furtive glances, I saw that unmistakable profile, a day or two's worth of unshaven beard, and a lone, renegade curl escaping the protection of his gray hood. Ironically, his disguise made him even more conspicuous; it was the height of summer, and everyone else was wearing warm-weather clothes.

He cooled himself with a cup of beer in each hand, looking around at the audience, taking sips, and sometimes nodding his head in time with the music. When he finished one beer, he slipped the full cup into the empty one. At one point, he looked to his right, facing my direction. Because of his impenetrable black shades, I wasn't sure exactly where he was looking, but I gave him a wide smile anyway. I hoped it would convey my feelings, since I had given up on the notion of approaching him. A million thoughts raced in my head; "Great show isn't it, Bob? The music is excellent, and it's a beautiful night. It's so cool that you're here. Don't worry, I'm not going to bother you." At first, his expression didn't change. But then the corners of his mouth turned up in a forced, yet polite, smile, almost as if he were reading my mind. Elated, I turned back to the music.

As the concert wound down and the crowd thinned out, Dylan approached three women in their mid-thirties standing five feet in front of me. They didn't seem to have noticed him before, but it was apparent they recognized him once he started talking. The topic was Johnny Winter's music, and Dylan appeared to be doing most of the talking. They didn't seem to be hard-core Dylan fans, and were very controlled while talking to him—listening to what he had to say, agreeing with him, and making their own interjections. He bummed a couple of cigarettes off one, and after several minutes, he said, "Well, it was nice talking to you, ladies. Have a good night," and turned to his bodyguards and walked away. Before departing, one of the bodyguards turned to us and said, "Thanks for not hassling him." Then they disappeared as quickly as they had appeared.

We stayed for another song before leaving the festival, but we were too excited to go home. So, we stopped off at one of the local college bars, where we met up with some friends who'd been at the Dylan concert, but had not been lucky enough to spot him in the crowd. "Good call," they said to me. I had to agree.

There's always an anticlimactic feeling that sets in after an exciting experience like this. At one point, I even began to wonder if it actually happened. Two days after the concert, the headline on the back page of the *Milwaukee Journal* read, "Who *was* that masked man in the crowd?" According to the article, others had spotted him walking along the festival grounds with his bodyguards. The column confirmed that he'd been there, and that I hadn't imagined it.

1989

No Time to Think

George O'Quinn, *47, currently works for the U. S. Department of Agriculture as Assistant Port Director in Fort Lauderdale, Florida.*

On November 15, 1989, I witnessed one of the 20-plus Bob Dylan concerts I've been fortunate enough to attend. I was working in Valdosta, Georgia, and had driven the four hours to Tampa, Florida, to meet friends at the show.

My date, who was not a true Dylan fan, suggested we leave after the first encore. Knowing I had another four-hour drive back to Valdosta and had to be at work bright and early the next morning, I grudgingly agreed. After saying our good-byes and heading back to our separate cars, I realized I was walking directly towards Dylan's tour bus, which was parked by the venue's exit. Casually, I strolled up and looked in the window leading to the concert hall. I was astounded to see Dylan at the end of a long hallway, walking alone and headed in my direction. As I stood dumbfounded, he approached the door, opened it, and walked toward the bus, where I was now standing.

When he was only a few feet away, all I could think to say was, "Thanks, Bob." He turned to look at me, grinned, and then bowed with his entire body. A bow to an anonymous fan, as if I were royalty.

That certainly made the night's eight hours of driving worthwhile.

1990

Tangled Up In Paparazzi

J. J. Stevens

"Another hit. Dylan snaps as cameras start to click," screamed the headlines in the *Daily Express*. "Who's got the hump?" questioned the *Daily Mirror* under a photograph of a man in dark glasses attempting to hide his face under a hooded leather coat. Many English Bob Dylan fans wondered what it was all about.

Well, now the story can be told by your man on the spot. Yes, I was there on that chilly Wednesday evening of February 7, 1990, outside the fashionable Mayfair Hotel in London. Bob Dylan was coming to the end of his six-night residency at the Hammersmith Odeon, where he had received rave reviews from both fans and critics for his performances in the relatively small venue.

It was 6:20 P.M. as I idled past the front entrance of the hotel on my way to nowhere in particular. I had already spotted a white Hertz van parked 50 yards away with two fold-up bicycles in the back. Knowing where our man had stayed in London in the past and his recent predilection for two-wheeled travel, it did not take the mind of a genius to put two and two together to figure out that he was inside this particular hotel. I reckoned there might be an infinitesimal chance of bumping into Bob and having him explain the mysteries of the universe to me in the 30 seconds it would take before his minders pounced on me. What I did not reckon on was seeing a group of 15 or so people, including photographers, blocking the entrance to the hotel.

Surely they were not all here for a close encounter with our man? Sure enough, they were not. That evening was to be the royal command performance of a Hollywood tear-jerker entitled *Steel Magnolias*. Several of the film's stars, including Olympia Dukakis, Julia Roberts, Sally Fields, and Daryl Hannah, were shortly to be whisked off by chauffeur-driven limousines to the film's premiere in Leicester Square, where they would be introduced to royalty. Now, Olympia, Sally, and company don't do much for me, but I had to admit to a certain prurient interest in viewing Daryl Hannah in the flesh. So I hung around with the gawkers, autograph hunters, and photographers to see what was about to go down.

Nothing happened for a while, and then I noticed a familiar face surveying the scene from another exit 20 yards away. It was Victor Maimudes, Dylan's erstwhile road manager and sparring partner from way back when. Precisely at this point, the affable cockney doorman at the Mayfair stepped out into the road to hail a passing taxi for a guest and was promptly knocked down by another car, whose driver had more urgent business. As it turned out, the doorman was not seriously hurt, but as he lay prostrate on the ground, I heard a voice behind me asking in a soft, American accent what had happened. I looked around to see Victor gazing over my shoulder at the unfortunate doorman. I explained what I had seen, and after a brief conversation in which he declared that there were "too many damned cars in this city," Victor strolled back into the hotel.

Attention now shifted to the hapless doorman who was helped to his feet and into the hotel. For 10 minutes or so, nothing much occurred, until I happened to glance toward the second exit and saw Victor coming out of the door accompanied by a familiar short figure wearing a thick leather jacket with a hood over his head and the usual pair of shades to hide his eyes. Also in evidence was a stocky male bodyguard and an attractive blonde woman in her early thirties wearing a peaked baseball cap. Suddenly, the strange group was spotted by several members of the throng gathered outside the main entrance. The people immediately rushed toward Dylan.

What happened next was curious. Dylan and his entourage had turned to the right upon leaving the hotel, even though their van was parked to the left. Now, to reach the van, the group had to do a complete turnabout and walk toward and through the crowd massed in front of the hotel. Once this turnaround occurred, Dylan's aide was unable to prevent a scrum of fans surging around the star, all pushing, shoving, and shouting out requests for Dylan to sign autographs here, there, and everywhere. With pen in hand, an impassive Dylan did indeed sign a few times; to be more precise, his hand carried out some jerky motions over bits of paper. Viewing one such autograph later, I saw that it bore absolutely no resemblance to "Bob Dylan" or any other name, for that matter.

With some assistance from Maimudes and the anonymous minder, Dylan eventually reached the comparative safety of the van's passenger seat, although eager photographers still gathered around him like vultures after a kill. Maimudes got into the van, started it up, and immediately reversed it into a parked Jaguar. This was faithfully recorded by the *Daily Express* reporter and her attendant photographer, although I do not recall that the license plate was damaged, as they later reported. The "mystery blonde" (certainly *not* Sally Kirkland, as another British newspaper said) and the bodyguard remained on the pavement. She was heard to say, "One or two autographs are okay, but this is ridiculous." I did not witness the van driving around the corner to Berkeley Square "at a snail's pace," as the *Daily Express* mentioned, nor did I see a "mean and moody" Bob Dylan assault a photographer with a rolled-up newspaper. It may have happened, although the photograph in the *Daily Express* purporting to show this incident looks decidedly dubious.

Why did Dylan choose this particular moment to use the main exit of the Mayfair Hotel, especially when there were two other exits where nobody would have spotted him? One of the hotel's doormen later told me he had never witnessed Bob using the main entrance until that day. Perhaps he was just a bit miffed at the lack of interest shown in him up to that point by the British press, or maybe he was a little jealous of some Hollywood stars stealing his limelight that evening.

1991

Too Much of Nothing

Anders Fajersson, *30, teaches high school English, Swedish, and history in Norrtalje, about 35 miles north of Stockholm.*

In the summer of 1991, Bob Dylan played a small theater in Stockholm called The Cirkus. It was beautiful; Bob was a bit tipsy and in a splendid mood, joking and dancing. After the gig, my friend and I were on such a high that we needed to celebrate. We headed for the Theater Bar for a beer, only to find that Columbia had rented it for an "invitation-only" post-gig party. American singer/songwriter Chris Whitley was scheduled to play for journalists and record company executives. Somehow, my friend and I managed to get past the bouncer. We headed directly to the bar, got a couple of beers, and walked out to the terrace.

A fellow approached and asked what we thought about the Dylan gig. I looked up and realized it was J. J. Jackson, Bob's guitarist. We talked for a while, and when he left, I told my friend, "We will probably never be closer to Bob Dylan than that." A few minutes later, Chris Whitley started to play, and we headed inside to watch his show.

Just then, Bob Dylan appeared at my side in the company of Tony Garnier, his bass player. I just had to talk to the man. I mean, this was Bob Dylan standing a foot or two away. Sadly, I had consumed a few too many by then, and my brain wasn't exactly at its sharpest.

I looked at him, and all I could think to say was, "Great show, Bob!"

The entire place went quiet, or so it felt anyway. Bobby looked at me, smiled, and said, "Whaddya mean *show*?"

I was dumbstruck. What did he mean, "Whaddya mean *show*?" Huh? Did I miss something, Bob? For some reason, he disapproved of the word "show," because of his strong emphasis on the word, almost as if it disgusted him or something. Tony Garnier was laughing his pants off as Bob propped one arm around his shoulder, and they sauntered off. There I stood, feeling like a complete idiot. Still, a couple of years down the road, I feel quite proud of my encounter in some weird way.

1992

Simple Twist of Fate

Anneke Hoftijzer *is a Gestalt Therapist from Hellevoetsluis, Holland. She met her husband, Hans Derksen, while waiting in line for a Bob Dylan concert. They maintain a small Dylan museum on the top floor of their home and host a web site devoted to collectors of Bob Dylan postcards and stamps,* www.fortunecity.com/tinpan/weekender/145/index.htm.

The first time I met Bob Dylan was on June 30, 1992, in Dunkirk, France. My sister and I were walking down the boulevard when a man suddenly grabbed me from behind by the shoulders and demanded that I "get rid of that guy." I turned around and discovered a very angry Bob Dylan. A young Belgian man was following him, snapping pictures as he walked down the street. He thought the man was with us. I assured Bob we didn't know the man, and while we speaking, the man took yet another picture. Bob apologized for bothering us and invited us to have a drink with him at the cafe *Espadrilles*. My sister asked him for his autograph, which he hesitantly gave, though he seemed a bit miffed by the request.

While in the cafe, Bob kept looking around nervously, because the place was filled with fans headed to the concert. But they behaved very politely and didn't bother us. Bob and I chatted about World War II, more specifically about the fighting that took place in Dunkirk. We talked about Holland (which is where I live) and the differences between being Jewish in the United States and being Jewish in Europe.

The author and the man in Dunkirk, France.

He admired the Chai pendant (Jewish symbol of life) around my neck. I even got up the nerve to ask him to do a better job that evening than he had at the Ultrecht, Holland, show in 1991, when he appeared to be drunk. He laughed, telling me he remembered the night very well.

We spoke for about 25 minutes, and then I left him alone as I realized that he wasn't just walking down the street that day solely to hang out with us. He's a very private man. We stood up from the table, and I said good-bye. He stood, looked me straight in the eyes, and said, "You know, I really like you." Then he kissed both my hands and bid us farewell. I have to say, it took me several weeks to get over it. I was so overwhelmed that I don't remember anything of the concert that evening. In fact, I don't even remember how I got home that night.

Amazingly, I met him again four years later, this time on a street corner in Madgeburg, Germany. He was wearing eyeglasses that were so ugly and odd looking that I couldn't help but laugh. I asked about his glasses, but he didn't say a word or even react to my question. He just stood there in silence, staring at me with those ridiculous glasses across his nose. Our standoff lasted about three minutes, with me laughing and Bob silently staring directly into my eyes. It was a very weird situation that made me uncomfortable, so I turned around and walked away.

1992

Most Likely You Go Your Way (and I'll Go Mine)

Mark Huff *has been Las Vegas' premier hometown singer/songwriter for more than a decade. With his gritty brand of blue-collar lyrics and rootsy rock & roll, he's been called the city's unsung answer to Dylan and Springsteen. His latest CD is* Skeleton Faith *[Exodus Records, 1140 S. 6th St., Las Vegas, NV 89104]. He can be reached through his web site at* www.markhuff.com.

My band, the Mark Huff Four, was hired to open for Bob Dylan at Bally's Hotel in Las Vegas in 1992. We arrived just in time to watch the afternoon sound check, but much to my disappointment, Bob didn't show up. His lead guitar player, J. J. Jackson, did all of the singing.

We went on at 8:15, and after a 45-minute set, we headed backstage. I knew Bob's band went on at 9:30, and I was dying to see them in action up close. When showtime finally rolled around and they headed for the stage, I decided to watch from the wings. Their performance that night was fantastic. I'd seen Bob play five nights at the Pantagious Theater in Hollywood in the previous week, so I expected they would do two encores and wasn't disappointed.

As the show came to a close, Bob and the band exited stage-left and headed for the backstage area. All night I'd been calculating the best time to approach Bob and introduce myself, and I figured now was it. I just had to meet him, but I also wanted to be really careful I didn't come across as some kind of weirdo. Because I was standing beside a table with a bunch of white towels on it, they all headed toward me. Bob walked right up beside me, grabbed a towel, and began wiping the sweat off his face.

Of course, I was completely awestruck, but eventually managed to mumble, "Hey, Bob. Great show." He looked at me and said, "Hey, thanks, man," and extended his hand to shake. I was so overcome with emotion for the man that, before I realized what I was doing, I gave him a big hug. It obviously caught him way off guard because his hand poked me right in my belly. Overall, he was very cool about the whole thing and began to pat my side with his hand. I got myself together somewhat and said, "You probably didn't see us, but we opened the show tonight; my name's Mark Huff. I really enjoyed your set."

He grinned and said, "Thanks, thanks a lot," and carried on with the task of wiping himself off with the towel.

Though the show had ended, I could still hear the audience clapping loudly in the background. His band began to circle around us like they were waiting to leave. Bob's road manager, Victor Maimudes, walked over and said, "C'mon, Bob, we're going out this way."

They all started walking toward the exit, and I remember thinking, "I'm just gonna hang out as long as I can." Victor, Bob, myself, some English chick, and a couple of guys from Dylan's band left through the back door, and that's when I saw the van. I thought, "Damn, they're all gonna get in and take off. This is the end of it." Thankfully, I was wrong.

MARK HUFF
SKELETON FAITH

Only the guys from Bob's band hopped in and split, leaving Bob, Victor, the British woman, and me standing outside.

As we walked down a ramp and through the back kitchen of Bally's Hotel, a million thoughts raced through my head, one of them being "They probably think I'm a complete freak or a real loser for hanging on like this." To say it was very awkward would be an understatement. But I wanted so much to hang out with Bob Dylan, and didn't know what else to do, that I kept walking with them.

Figuring I'd better make some light conversation quick, I said to Bob, "Hey, by the way, I'm friends with your son-in-law Peter Himmelman."

Bob replied, "Oh yeah?"

"Yeah, I've played with him a couple of times."

"Well, that's awwriiight," Bob said quietly.

That walk seemed like an eternity, though in reality it was only about three minutes. Finally, we arrived at the service elevator. Victor opened it, and the three of them stepped in, leaving only me standing there.

Bob spoke up, "All right, man, I gotta go now."

Of course, this was the signal that the moment had arrived to say my good-byes to him. "Hey, Bob, it was really great meeting you."

He smiled and said, "I'll see you around, man."

Once again he extended his hand, and this time I shook it instead of hugging him. The elevator doors closed as I watched the man disappear from view. I picked up my guitar case and made my way slowly back up the ramp. Nights like those don't roll around too often.

1994

Sign Language

Masato Kato, *33, is a teacher who lives in Kanagawa, Japan.*

When Dylan toured Japan in February 1994, I decided to see most of the shows. I started by taking a bullet train from Kokura to Hiroshima on the morning of February 16.

Around noon, my friends and I went to the hotel where we thought Dylan would stay. Our guess was right. At 2:28 P.M., Dylan, dressed in a long, black coat, and his entourage arrived at the hotel. We started to approach, but as soon as he saw us, he quickly disappeared into the elevator. We were lucky enough, though, to meet his guitarist, J. J. Jackson, and pedal steeler/violinist Bucky Baxter and get their autographs.

As we sat in the hotel lobby waiting for Dylan to reappear, a big man with an angry face approached and ordered me to stand. I did as I was told. As soon as he seated himself on the sofa and told me to sit back down, however, he flashed us a smile. We learned he was "Big Jim" Callahan, Bob's bodyguard. After giving us his name, the next words he spoke were, "You people should know that Bob never meets his fans and never signs autographs."

Later, I wound up escorting Big Jim to Hiroshima Peace Park while the others waited for Dylan to come down to the hotel lobby. Big Jim asked a lot of questions about Japanese history, and I somehow managed to answer all of them. He told me he was a year old when the first atomic bomb exploded in Hiroshima.

At 5:35 P.M., Dylan left for the concert hall. Needless to say, Big Jim didn't allow us to meet him. All we could do was stand helplessly and watch as he climbed into the black van. When I noticed Bob looking at us, I waved. To our delight, Dylan returned the wave.

After the concert, we went to the hotel restaurant for supper. As we ate, Bucky, J. J., Tony Garnier, and Big Jim entered the restaurant and began drinking at a table near us. Shortly thereafter, a strange woman with a '70s Yoko Ono hairstyle approached and tried to speak to them in Japanese. Big Jim called to me, "Hey, Kato. Would you come over here and help us out?"

He asked me to interpret for the woman, who, it turned out, wanted to give Dylan a present. After supper, Big Jim and J. J. invited us to join them at the bar, but we said our goodnights because it was very late.

We returned to the hotel at 9:30 the next morning. J. J., Tony, and Big Jim were on their way to Hiroshima Peace Park, so we decided to join them. Later that evening, we returned to the hotel. While sitting in the lobby, we saw Dylan, accompanied by a young man and woman, stroll out of the elevator and head toward the main entrance/exit of the hotel. When we tried to follow him, Big Jim stopped us. We later learned the people with him were his son and daughter, and that they were headed to Hiroshima Peace Park.

When they returned that evening, Big Jim finally allowed us to approach Bob, who was wearing a light-gray hooded jacket and sunglasses. I told him I had traveled all the way to New York City to celebrate his 30th anniversary in October 1992. He looked very impressed and said, "Oh, good," with that certain drawl of his. I saw his eyebrows move behind his sunglasses.

The strange woman with the Yoko Ono hair then came up and presented Bob with a gift (an ashtray) and a letter. Bob took the ashtray and began to read the letter. She had written "I love you" nearly 30 times. That was the entire content of the letter. Including us, there were 10 fans standing there, and everyone got to say hello and shake hands with Bob. His hand was very soft and his fingernails quite long. I thought my moment with Dylan was over and started to walk off when he asked me to interpret for the strange woman who had given him the gift and letter. He asked her questions such as, "Where do you come from?," "What does your father do?," and "Do you like to travel?" It was truly one of the happiest moments in my life.

Three years later, on February 22, 1997, I encountered Bob again after a splendid show in Akita. Three friends and I went to the hotel where he and his band were staying, although we didn't expect to meet Dylan again. We were just waiting for J. J., Bucky, Tony, or drummer David Kemper to return from the hotel bar. Suddenly, Bob appeared in the lobby. He had just come back from a night walk with Fred, his new bodyguard and dresser. Bob seemed to be in a very upbeat mood and had a great smile. Four of us managed to shake his hand and exchange a couple of words.

I asked, "Do you remember we met in Hiroshima?"

Bob replied, "Oh sure, that's right. Yeah, I remember."

I'm sure Bob frequently replies this way when asked that kind of question, so I don't know if he really remembered me. But I was still very excited to meet him again and see that beautiful smiling face. He disappeared before we had a chance to ask for his autograph.

Finally, I had a great time taking a walk with Bob's guitar tech in Akita. He was a very good guy with a lot of knowledge about rock and roll and computers. We visited some record stores and computer shops, and he bought me a cup of coffee. I also met J. J. Jackson, Tony Garnier, and Bucky Baxter again. And, in Sapparo, as a "Deadhead" I was especially happy to meet David Kemper, a former drummer in the Jerry Garcia Band. We talked about Dylan and Garcia and their inspiring music. Bob Dylan, his band, and crew were (and are) all great people.

1994

I'll Keep It With Mine

Michael Cramer *is a 25-year-old financial analyst for a hedge fund who lives in New York City.*

I'm a huge fan of Bob Dylan and decided, for whatever reason, to get a tattoo of him. In August 1994, I chose the famous image of him in London from 1965 (from the *Don't Look Back* period) and had it engraved on my leg in black ink. It came out really well, and the woman who did it asked that I send her a picture once it healed. So, my father took a few shots, and we sent it off to her.

Two months later, Dylan played the Orpheum Theater in Boston, and I drove home to see the show with a good friend and my dad. After finding our seats, dad pulled out an envelope containing one of the photos of my tattoo, a self-addressed stamped envelope, and a letter that read:

Dear Mr. Dylan,

My son is a tremendous fan of yours. This past summer, he had your face tattooed on his leg. Is there any way you could sign the enclosed picture and return it to him in the enclosed envelope?

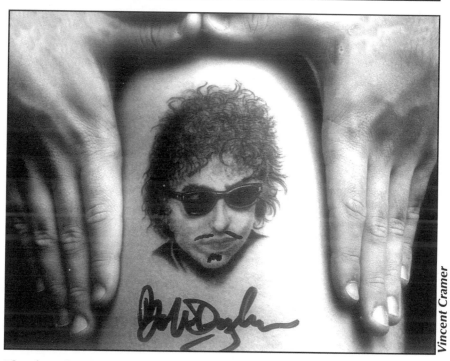

Vincent Cramer

The signed and altered photograph of the author's leg tattoo.

I told him he was crazy and that it was never going to work. But he didn't listen. He walked up to one of the ushers working near the stage, explained the entire story, and asked him to get the letter to Dylan backstage somehow. The usher laughed and said he would do his best.

Two days later, the self-addressed envelope arrived at my house. Inside was the photo with Bob's signature across the bottom and a hand-drawn goatee and mustache across his face. It's certainly one of the most unique souvenirs I've ever seen, and I'll treasure it forever.

1994

Going, Going, Gone

Monte A. Melnick, *49, was the tour manager for the Ramones from 1976 through 1997. He currently coordinates special events for artists such as Ronnie Spector; Joey, Dee Dee, and Marky Ramone; Paul Winter; and D Generation.*

The year was 1994, and the Ramones had just released *Acid Eaters*, an album of their favorite tunes from the '60s and '70s. One of the songs they covered was Bob Dylan's "My Back Pages."

At the time, I was their tour manager, and we often held rehearsals at S.I.R. Studios on West 25th Street in New York City. S.I.R. is a large rehearsal facility, and most major musical talents use it to practice when in town.

It was late afternoon and we were standing in the lobby when we noticed a small figure walk in looking very nervous and uncomfortable. Staying close to the wall, he slunk into one of the rehearsal rooms. To our amazement, it was none other than Bob Dylan. Being big Dylan fans, we were all excited by this discovery. After some debate, we decided to send a couple of copies of *Acid Eaters* in with a crew member, with a request for one to be autographed. Sometime later, the crew member returned and informed us that Bob Dylan doesn't sign anything. We were all pretty disappointed but not totally surprised.

Several months later, the Ramones were on tour in Japan and had a night off in Tokyo. That same evening, Dylan was playing at The Budokan, and, luckily, we were able to get tickets. After enjoying the concert, we made our way backstage, where to the surprise of Joey Ramone, Dylan approached him and said, "Hey, how ya' doin', Joey?"

Joey was astonished that Dylan had come directly up to him. After collecting himself, he asked Bob what he thought of the Ramones' version of "My Back Pages." Dylan looked up at Joey and gave him a huge smile. Then, quick as lightning, he was whisked away by his management into a private dressing room.

Such was our encounter with the mysterious Bob Dylan.

1995

Boots of Spanish Leather

Quino Castro, *32, is a professional photographer employed by the press department of Estepa, a small city in the province of Sevilla, Spain. He estimates he has seen Dylan in concert 35 times since his sister introduced him to Bob's music in 1978. He is also the leader of the Dark Eyes Electric Band.*

Amparo, Jesus, and I were on Bob Dylan's trail in my car for the 1995 Spain tour. We'd thoroughly enjoyed the first concert in Bilbao, where we heard a wonderful version of "Born in Time" and saw a more communicative Dylan than usual. Now we were in Madrid for the second show, and everything indicated we would enjoy a very special night at *Sala La Riviera*, the intimate 2,500-seat venue.

By waiting at the door for three or four hours, we managed to get seats in the first row, near the center of the stage. There were rumors that Dylan had entered the building by the front door, right in front of all of us lined up to go in, wearing a dark jacket with a hood that covered his face. Once we got inside, I realized the small barrier and short distance between the first row and the low stage increased the possibility of shaking his hand or at least making eye contact.

The concert began, and Bob didn't wait to direct glances at the first row, blowing a kiss to a blonde girl on the left. Such was the girl's passion that at the end of the concert, she jumped up onstage. Bob himself went to her rescue when she was detained by security bouncers, and when he went backstage, she was allowed to go with him. She returned to the audience after the first encore. After each subsequent encore, Bob shook hands with the first row, as is his custom when contented with the show and the audience. (He smiled throughout the entire concert.) Jesus touched Bob's boots, and Amparo even received his gaze on the last "babe" of "It Ain't Me, Babe," something he habitually did when he spotted a girl in the first row. I was in a strategic position to touch him but smothered by the crowd pushing to get near. I decided this would be the moment to get the desired autograph.

"Like a Rolling Stone" had just ended when I borrowed a pen from Jesus and began searching desperately for a piece of paper. I knew Bob would pay no attention to someone showing him a pen and piece of scrap paper. We already knew he doesn't like signing autographs, so I began to search for something more unique. In my wallet, I found a printed image of a painting of Jesus Christ crucified that I'd been saving for years. Instead of requesting an autograph, I showed the picture of Christ to Bob. He was shaking hands with the young people in the first row when he saw me holding up my print of Christ. He looked into my face, and his expression changed. We could see surprise and confusion in his eyes. I can only imagine what must have passed through his mind when he saw an unknown person in the audience showing him the visage of Christ in a picture. I'm sure he pondered the purpose of the act. To this day, I believe he'd have denied me the autograph had Jesus' picture not been on the paper.

He took the print and stepped back, at which point I began yelling out my request for an autograph. Suddenly, I felt the press of the multitude against me, and one of the protective barriers broke. I boldly decided to climb up onto the stage. Thanks to my friend Fredy and an Italian guy named Alexandro, who helped me up, I was able to approach Bob.

I found myself at his side and handed him my pen. With a gesture, he indicated he thought the print of Christ was for him and not for an autograph. I answered with gestures that said, "Fine, do what you want." He grabbed the pen and tried to sign over Christ's face, but the print was

in plastic and impossible to write on. I indicated he should sign on the back and, almost illegibly, he signed it with a "BD." For me, the autograph was less important than the fact that this person who so often inspired me was standing right beside me and had dedicated a few moments of his time to me. I had one eye on Bob and the other on the security guys, who surprisingly did not intervene when they saw he had agreed to sign.

The seconds that I stood beside Bob Dylan were very profound. I remember a peculiar odor filled my senses, a mixture of perfume and sweat. When Dylan returned the autographed picture and pen to me, I was very nervous. He gestured in appreciation, to which I answered with a sincere "Thanks a lot, Bob." He retired, only to reappear for one final encore of "Rainy Day Women." I remained onstage during the last song since my place in the audience had been rapidly filled by fans.

In hindsight, even though it was very emotional for me at the moment, I realize now it was a little forward to invade the stage and approach Bob in that way. Today, I don't think it would be so important to have Bob's autograph. Any of his songs listened to at the right moment with the person you love can be a moment more important than all others.

One More Weekend

Al Lopez *is a retired contract programmer who says Dylan has been a part of the rhythm of his life since being introduced to his music in 1965.*

It was noon on Saturday, May 25, 1995, when I steered my car out of the lot of the Buffalo Motel in Jamestown, North Dakota, and headed east on Highway 94. Low, rolling hills straddled each side of the highway, with an occasional farmhouse interspersed between fields of crops imbedded with hay and grain. My focus, though, was not on sundry matters, but on my pilgrimage to Bob Dylan's hometown of Hibbing, Minnesota—Mecca for any Dylan devotee.

While driving, I began to ponder the interlacing of Dylan's music with my own movement through life, beginning in 1964 when his music was first introduced to me. The woman who opened my eyes to his genius was an artist who worked in the department next to mine. One day she approached me and asked, "Have you ever heard of a singer named Bob Dylan? He's really incredible."

That was enough to spur me on. I bought a couple of his albums and was soon launched into years of "Dylan Mania." "Listen to the words" became my oft-repeated cry to those poor souls still unaware of the sheer power of his poetry.

At Fargo, I turned north and picked up Highway 10 through town and on into Minnesota. As I headed further east, the scenery began to change, and I was soon engulfed in wooded hills sprinkled with multi-colored signs indicating the nearest resort lakes, golf courses, and fishing and camping spots. By then, I'd gone through my fourth Dylan cassette tape and found myself slowly drifting into an introspective, almost hypnotic state. I sifted through the memories flashing across my mind, reflecting on how it seemed that Bob Dylan's music had always been there coloring some of the most important moments of my life.

• She was working the switchboard in my office back in 1968 when I handed her the words to "Love Minus Zero/No Limit." "Oh, that's really good," she said to me after reading them. The switchboard girl later became the love of my life to whom I'm still married.

• The Forum in Los Angeles, 1974, my two daughters beside me as we lit matches and swayed together to Dylan's closing number, "Like a Rolling Stone."

Only 30 miles to go now. I stopped to buy a Dylan tape I'd apparently left at home. Settling in once again behind the wheel and cranking up the volume to "Like a Rolling Stone," I turned left onto the main loop road through town. I remember wondering, "Where are all the signs reading, HOME OF BOB DYLAN? Why aren't any of the shops selling Dylan paraphernalia? Don't they get it?"

Finally, justice at last. At a motel off the highway outside of town, I discovered a huge map with little buttons showing local points of interest. One indicated the location of the house where Dylan grew up. "Wowee, paydirt," I almost yelled out loud. Strangely, right next to the "Bob's boyhood home" button was one indicating the biggest hole ever dug by man. Well, one has to balance things out.

After viewing Dylan's childhood home, Hibbing High School, and the surrounding neighborhood, I ended up on a stool at Zimmy's Place, a local

Above: Bob's boyhood home. Below: Zimmy's Place, where Hibbing's elite meet to greet each other and celebrate the city's most famous citizen.

pub that was like an orchid growing in the middle of Antarctica. An entire wall was lined with Bob Dylan posters, and the clientele was certainly receptive to my weaving him in with various other topics of conversation. It was an incredible evening, as I chatted freely with the locals about my hero and the complexities of life.

The most peculiar part of my visit to Zimmy's was the band that played the evening set. They didn't know a single Bob Dylan tune and proceeded to play '50s numbers until the crowd thinned out. A fresh-faced, young girl from the north country nudged me onto the dance floor, where we be-bopped to "Wooly Bully."

I reluctantly packed my bags the next morning, wishing that I could stay on for just a few more days. My pilgrimage to Hibbing was something I knew I'd been destined to make for many long years. Now, I feel I can die happily ever after.

1995

Sweetheart Like You

Lee Parham, *53, is a musician and personal assistant who met Jenny Langley, 36, in 1985 at a biker bar he once owned in Barnesville, Georgia. Jenny was the first person in that state to prove that living at home was less expensive than living in a nursing home, which resulted in the establishment of the state's Independent Care Waiver Program. Lee and Jenny are currently building their own home in McDonough, Georgia.*

The date was October 11, 1995. The place was Atlanta's Fox Theater. After arriving at the theater, we had a hassle with the ushers because of my friend Jenny's wheelchair (she's quadriplegic). We had front-row tickets, and by gosh, we were going to sit in the front row. After much grumbling from the staff, we made them move a chair and put her wheelchair in place, which placed us about four feet from the stage.

Bob came out dressed in a gold shirt with the tail out, a black leather belt with conches, black pants with stripes down the sides, and square-toe boots. When he began to play his sunburst Fender Stratocaster, electricity ran through our blood from just being that close to someone we admired so much. For the first four songs, he never looked up from his

Lee Parham

Jenny Langley with Bob's flowers.

guitar. Then he stepped back, took a long drink of water, and looked out at the audience. We caught his eye immediately, and for the remainder of the concert Bob looked directly at us on numerous occasions.

As the show wound to a close, the previously vigilant ushers (who'd been so concerned that everyone was in their proper seats) allowed everyone to rush the stage. We pushed our way up to the point where Jenny's footrest was flush against the front of it. Bob broke into "Seeing the Real You at Last," and the band locked into an intense groove. There were so many people in the orchestra pit that the wooden floor began to bounce furiously. During the frantic finish, I had to throw my arm across Jenny to keep her from bouncing right out of her wheelchair.

Following the encore, Bob picked up a bouquet of beautiful spring flowers at his feet that someone had thrown onstage. He walked from one end of the stage to the other, holding them high in the air and taking his bows. When he reached our side of the stage, he strolled up to Jenny and looked her directly in the eyes. Gesturing with the bouquet in his hands, he said, "Would you like to have these?"

Jenny, smiling from ear to ear, vigorously nodded her head and screamed out, "*Yes*." Bob handed me the bouquet to pass on to her and gave me a high-five. Jenny yelled out, "Thank you, Bob."

At the close of the second encore, Bob once again strolled the stage taking his bows. Just as he was walking off for the last time, he turned to look and walked back toward us again. Grabbing my right hand, he shook it firmly and said, "You're all right, man."

As the houselights came on and people began milling out onto Peachtree Street, several concert-goers came up to Jenny, saying, "Wow, Bob Dylan gave you flowers. Congratulations."

Jenny brought those beautiful flowers home that night, and, after taking a quick snapshot of her holding them to her chest, we hung them up to dry. Only then did the impact of what actually took place begin to sink in. Those flowers now hang in Jenny's bedroom as a reminder of that very special evening.

Bob Dylan seems to speak of feelings we all have about life, death, and the bitter sweetness of love, and we somehow find comfort in his words. For us, it was an experience we'll never forget, and Bob Dylan will never realize the impact he made on Jenny's life that night.

Mixed-up Confusion

Josh Nicols

I'm a 16-year-old hardcore Bob Dylan fan who saw his first show at the end of 1996 at Buffalo Bill's in Jean, Nevada. It was a really great show because everyone rushed the stage and I got to see Brother Bob from about five feet away.

Afterwards, my friend and I stood outside by his tour bus and waited for him to come out. When we finally saw him exit the building, we screamed out, "Hey, Zimmy! You gotta serve somebody."

He turned around to look at us and mumbled something that sounded like "Fuzzah aroo jumbay."

Heck, we had absolutely no idea what he said, but we cheered anyway. We had made contact with the greatest singer of all time.

1996

She Belongs to Me

Jamie Peterson

I'm the 49-year-old mother of two college-aged kids. I've loved and followed Bob Dylan since I was a girl of 14. The first time I saw him perform was in Minneapolis, back in 1964.

My kids grew up listening to my Dylan albums, though they never seemed really moved by his music. When they were in grade school, I took them to his outdoor concert at Harriet Island in St. Paul, hoping to get them interested. Sadly, the most excitement they registered all evening was when they spotted the food vendors.

Around the time my daughter turned 16, she discovered that Dylan was scheduled to play the Target Center in Minneapolis. Needless to say, I was both shocked and pleased when she asked me to accompany her to the concert. We had a complete ball. By the time Bob started singing "The Times They Are A-Changin'," both of us were dancing around like madwomen. I remember thinking how strange it seemed that Dylan had been a part of my life even longer than her.

The Target Center concert really did the trick for my daughter. Immediately, she began wearing the Dylan tee shirt purchased at the show. She also confiscated one of my posters for her room and began sneaking my tapes and CDs. She even forced her girlfriends to watch *Don't Look Back*, the documentary of Dylan's 1965 English tour.

One year later, in November 1996, she burst into my office and ecstatically relayed the news that Bob would once again play the Midwest, and that we had to buy our tickets right away. I was thrilled with the realization I had indeed done my job right in raising her. I took off from work and she took off from school, and we wound up catching three concerts in one unforgettable week—Milwaukee, Wisconsin; Mankato, Minnesota; and Davenport, Iowa.

At the Mankato show, we somehow managed to make it up to the front of the stage. The crowd was the usual can of sardines, but it still felt great to be there. I was just dancing around minding my own business, when I looked up and saw my daughter strutting across the stage toward Bob. I couldn't believe my eyes. She appeared so casual and cool as she strolled right up to him, gave him a big hug, and planted a kiss right smack on his lips. Dylan just smiled, nodded his head, and kept right on playing his guitar. My sweet little girl then turned and faced the crowd of thousands, gave a couple of big thumbs-up signals, and dove headfirst back into the audience.

As if that wasn't enough to give me heart failure, I suddenly felt a couple of teenage guys lift and toss me up onstage. Petrified, I landed directly in front of Dylan in a heap, with my skirt up around my neck. Immediately, a "gentleman" working security grabbed me by the back of my sweater and skirt and swung me right back into the crowd. It was quite unnerving, to say the least.

When the concert ended, a literal mob of teenagers surrounded my daughter to congratulate and hug her for having actually kissed Bob Dylan. I'll never forget overhearing my 16-year-old child casually describe our then 55-year-old hero to this envious group of girls as an "absolute darling."

Since that night, this girl has been *my* hero.

1997

It's Alright Ma, (I'm Only Reading)

Dale Foster, *43, is an Information Systems professor at Memorial University in St. Johns, Newfoundland.*

My parents, who are in their late sixties, were visiting for Easter when Bob Dylan played our hometown, St. John's, Newfoundland, on April 1, 1997. Although they weren't particularly big Dylan fans, my husband and I bought tickets for them and asked them to accompany us.

Mom used to make fun of Dylan's "nasally" voice and make mother-like comments whenever we played his records on the living room hi-fi, the only record player in the house. Still, her comments were always in good humor, and to our delight, they enjoyed the concert tremendously.

As they were preparing to fly home the following day, mom spotted Dylan sitting in the airport's very small departure lounge. He was flying back on the same flight as they. She approached and asked him point blank, "Excuse me, sir. Are you Bob Dylan? If so, would you please autograph my concert ticket?"

He cautiously looked up from his newspaper and said, "Were you at my concert? You look as old as me."

A bit taken aback, she confirmed that she and my father had indeed seen the show, and that, in fact, she was probably older than he. He agreed to give his autograph and waited patiently while mom struggled to retrieve a pen from my dad. Bob signed her ticket and then walked over to return the pen to my father. What a gracious gentleman. It sure made her day, and I was impressed all to pieces that my very own mother spoke with Bob Dylan.

154

Long Island University, 1989.

1997

Got My Mind Made Up

Robin Pickens

On October 24, 1997, my boyfriend and I drove to Mobile, Alabama, from our home in west central Illinois to see a Bob Dylan concert. The show was general admission, so anyone who arrived early had the opportunity to get awesome seats. We got there two hours before the doors opened and managed to get second row. Finally, Bobby appeared onstage at 8:00 P.M., and the party began.

About halfway through the concert, a man in his early twenties tapped me on the shoulder. Observing my camera, he asked if I would snap a picture of Bob for him. Once I did, and he had given me his address so I could mail the photo to him, he proceeded to chat about the many concerts that he'd attended. Then he said he was planning to jump onstage after Bob finished the song he was playing, which was "Just Like a Woman." With only one row of people in front of us, he figured he couldn't lose. Unfortunately, the folks in front of us were real jerks; they not only wouldn't let him through, but they ratted him out to the security guard. We tried to explain to the guard that people often get onstage at Dylan shows, but to no avail. This upset me to the point of tears because I had been planning my *own* little onstage encounter with Bob. If the folks in front of us wouldn't let the guy through, I knew I was doomed, too.

The fellow that so desperately wanted onstage didn't give up though; he just moved down the row near some nicer people. They let him through just as Bob was walking off stage, signaling the end of the show. The lights were down, but I could see that his quest was over; he'd made it to Dylan. A crew member tried to intercept him, but it was too late, and Bob shook the young man's hand.

After seeing this guy make it onstage, I decided I could do it, too. So, I moved down to the spot where he got though and informed the people around me that I was also going up. Just then, Dylan returned to play an encore, and I tried to climb up, but fell. Thankfully, it appeared no one noticed. He left shortly after that, only to come back out and play two more songs. After I heard the last few bars of "Rainy Day Women," I knew my time had come. I grabbed the shoulders of the two gentlemen on either side of me and hoisted myself to the top of the barrier and stepped up onto the stage. I was so nervous, I thought I would pass out. There I was onstage with *Bob Dylan.*

When I stepped up, he had his back to me, so I began to walk toward him. Just then, he turned around and headed back toward the microphone. This made me think he was about start playing another song, and I had to do some quick thinking. I knew it would be rude to stand in front of him while he was trying to play. Out of politeness, I sat down on the stage. Seconds later, Dylan noticed me sitting there and made a noise of surprise, followed with an "Oh?" He smiled and put his hand down, as if he wanted to give me five. I smacked my hand against his and stood up. Taking one step toward him, I opened my arms and said, "Bob, I just have to hug you." Again, he smiled, and then did the unexpected and embraced me. To say I was in complete shock would be the understatement of my life. Afterwards, thinking that security might be along any minute to haul me away, I turned and jumped off the stage, back into the crowd.

It was the happiest moment of my entire life, and I really hope to do it again sometime soon.

1997

What Can I Do For You?

Deborah Avis Wall, *35, is a product designer and the owner of Sparrow's Mandolin Outfitter, an internet-based business. She has been a songwriter and performing/recording musician for nearly 20 years and a Bob fan for as long as she can remember.*

It was a scraggly man in old jeans and a hooded sweatshirt who walked into Wuxtry Records in Athens, Georgia, on Monday night, October 26, 1997. Although Wuxtry is well-known in the states and internationally, it maintains a charming "mom and pop" feel. I suppose that's part of the reason that Bob Dylan did a "pop-in" on the evening before his first Athens show.

The man didn't look much different from some of the normal clientele, so I went about my computer work in the back of the store as usual. Immediately, the man sniffed out the store's great vinyl section, where he spotted a Buck Owens LP on the display wall. Unable to read the price tag because the album was too high up on the wall, he came to the front of the store to ask a clerk. Summoned to answer the stranger's question, I brought a step stool from the back. It was obvious it was going to be a real task to move record crates just to get a look.

So, I said to the stranger, who was flipping through the country LP crates with his back turned to me, "If you're really interested in this thing, I'll get it down. But if you're just curious. . ."

Just then, the kid working with me came to the back and volunteered to climb up and check the price of the record. Naturally, after all that, the album was unmarked. The stranger mumbled something to the effect of, "Aw, that's all right, don't go worrying about it," and went on flipping through the records.

Some 15 minutes later, I took a break and joined my co-worker in the front, where he quietly whispered, "Deb, did you get a look at that guy? I'm not sure, but I think it might be Bob Dylan."

The instant he said that, I looked over at the man and realized he was right. That explained the pulled-up hood nearly closed around his face and why he didn't turn around and talk to me about the Buck Owens record. And the voice was unmistakable. We left Dylan alone in the back with the LPs, where he seemed to be genuinely enjoying himself. Out of respect, we kept folks away from him and did not intrude ourselves. Eventually, he emerged and walked to the front of the store, where he met us head-on.

Inside the hood of his sweatshirt was that face that could only belong to Bob Dylan. He was very friendly and inquisitive about our merchandise, and he wanted to know where we kept the CDs and LPs of Georgia blues artists. We talked about some of the records we had in stock, and I showed him a "Barbeque Bob" record that got a chuckle out of him. Not because he found "Barbeque Bob" to be a joke, but because I had used the name Bob. I'm sure he was aware I knew who he was, but he might have been a bit perplexed because I wasn't nervous or freaking out on him. I said the name "Bob," and we both knew that's who he was.

I knew that talking about music with Bob Dylan was an important event in my life, but at Wuxtry we've all experienced the famous musician shopper at one time or another. We like to take the respect angle rather than the star-struck one. He was just so comfortable with us, which I found very unlike anything I'd ever heard about Bob. He came to the front counter, and leaning over the glass display case, began to ask about the new Jim

Mathus release (the guy from the Squirrel Nut Zippers). We had a promo copy, so I put it on for him and we listened to a good part of it. He commented on the recording quality, saying it was "old-timey sounding." He studied the cover art and asked questions about who had played on the record. All the while, he was petting the store mascot, Bentley, a 15-year-old poodle. At one point, Bob winked at him and said, "You're okay, old man."

I offered him the promotional CD, but he declined, saying he might come back for it. He thanked us for playing it and wished us a good evening. Then he nudged back the hood of his sweatshirt just enough to reveal his face in the light, flashed a big grin, and walked out into the night.

> *"Bob Dylan is a figure that arises every 300 or 400 years, who represents and embodies all the finest aspirations of the human heart. He is unparalleled in the world of music and will remain a torch for all singers and all hearts for many generations to come."*
>
> *—**Leonard Cohen***

Open the Door, Dylan

Kate Anschuetz, *44, is a confidential secretary for the state of Michigan's Children's Protective Services. She is married with two children, ages 24 and 19. Her friend Jill is a computer technician for the same agency.*

Over the long 1998 Memorial Day weekend, my friend Jill and I decided to take a trip to Minnesota from our hometown in northern Michigan. Because I'm a Dylan fan and Jill is a Judy Garland fan, we incorporated stops in Hibbing (Bob's hometown) and Grand Rapids (Garland's birthplace) into our itinerary. This was to be our first road trip together, and for the trip, Jill and I dubbed ourselves "The Seatcovers, Inc.," a trucker/CB term for women in vehicles. She was Gypsy Jill and her Traveling Tamborine, and I was Kate the Great, the Queen of Everything.

We'd done our homework on the Internet, gathering information on places to visit in our idols' hometowns and sights in and around Minneapolis. In my research, I came across a posting on a message board where the question was asked, "Has anyone out there found Dylan's farm in Hanover, Minnesota, yet?" I didn't even know he had a farm, and there was no answer posted. Checking the map, I discovered Hanover is only a short drive northwest of Minneapolis, so we added it to our travel plans.

On a beautiful, sunny Saturday, May 23, we set out to find Hanover. With a map in hand, we thought we knew the way. It wasn't long, however, before we discovered that the small county road we were looking for didn't exist. At least, we couldn't find it. Eventually, we took a road leading north, hoping it would get us in the vicinity. Fifteen minutes later, just as we were about to give up and turn around, we spotted a sign that said: Welcome to Hanover. Talk about dumb luck.

We drove first one way through the small community, then another, catching sight of more than a few mailboxes with "Zimmerman" printed on the side. We finally stopped for a drink at a place called the Hilltop Tavern, where we scrutinized some of the patrons' faces, imagining them to be Dylan's cousins. We even discussed the possibility that Bob himself might walk through the door. Eventually, Jill screwed up the courage to ask the bartender if he knew the location of Dylan's farm.

"Sure," came his reply, and he proceeded to give detailed directions and warn us about the caretaker. "Be careful," he advised. "He's really mean." A waitress walked past as he said this and responded, "Oh, he is not. He's a pushover." That was all the encouragement we needed.

We followed the bartender's directions and found ourselves at the entrance to a long, unremarkable driveway. We turned in and drove past the home we assumed from the directions to be the place. A short distance past that was a cottage we believed belonged to the caretaker. We stopped in front of the cottage, where we were met by a rather large German shepherd. After making his acquaintance and deciding he was friendly, Jill got out and knocked on the door. No answer. She knocked again...still no reply.

We drove to the end of the driveway, stopping in front of a huge, two-story white house. To our left was a large expanse of lawn with a tennis court. There were several buildings (homes?) scattered on the perimeter of the property. The white house in front of us was massive, with a white stucco-type exterior and a wrap-around balcony on the second floor. We approached the door calling out, "Hello? Anyone home?" We didn't want to startle anyone, although it turned out there was no one there to hear us except the overly friendly German shepherd and a meandering Calico cat. Meandering looked like the thing to do; we continued to search for the caretaker.

We never did find him, or anyone else for that matter, but careful peeks through the windows confirmed that this house did indeed belong to Bob Dylan. Inside the front door was a coat rack with a couple of jackets and three very Dylan-style hats hanging on top. On the wall, next to the coat rack, was a painting of a younger Bob. The wall in the living area faced the backyard and was topped with stained glass that ran the length of the room.

To the right was a bookcase extending the length of the wall, filled with books on Judaism and Picasso, amongst others. A chess set was nestled on a lower shelf. The jackpot was located on the bottom left of the bookcase—Dylan albums, including *Biograph*, which we could plainly read on the album spine. By this point, I was in total awe, not to mention a little concerned that should someone come upon us, we might find ourselves in a heap of trouble. We were trying hard not to disturb anything and be as unobtrusive as possible.

Located slightly behind and to the left of the main house was a smaller building with a redwood exterior. Several windows were shuttered from inside. Of course, we had to take a look here, too, assuming it was the guest house. However, the first window we looked through made clear it was no guest house, but a music studio. In the room on the left were two keyboards, a small drum set, and a xylophone. The room in the middle contained a very old, well-traveled guitar case, recording equipment, and reel-to-reel tapes. I could only imagine who might be on those tapes, besides Mr. Dylan, of course.

We'd been there approximately 45 minutes by then and decided not to push our luck further. Before leaving, however, we had one more thing to do. Since the next day, May 24th, was Bob's birthday, we had brought along a birthday card. We opened the screen door of the music studio and left the card between the doors, with the hope the finder would pass it on to Bob. Or better yet, that Bob would find it himself.

Jill wasn't a Dylan fan before this excursion to Minneapolis, but on the 14-hour trip home, all she wanted to hear was every Dylan tape I'd brought. We were fortunate to stumble across the question about the farm over the Internet. We were luckier still to have had the opportunity to actually find it. It's a trip neither of us will ever forget.

1998

Positively 4th Street

Janet Fleming *is a purchasing agent and a mother of four from Chicago. She saw her first Dylan concert in 1965, when she was 16, and says it changed her life forever. Still, she saw him only once more, in 1976, between that first show and 1997, when her youngest daughter asked to attend a Dylan concert for her 15th birthday. Since then, she has attended 22 Dylan concerts, many with her daughter, and says she expects see at least 22 more.*

The Olympia Airport bus emerged from the Lincoln Tunnel, enroute to Newark Airport. Off to my left was the New York City skyline. I was sad to be leaving but anxious to get home and share my adventures and feelings with those I knew would understand. As I looked at the glittering skyline, I thought, "Bob Dylan has come full circle. He's back in New York, singing and strumming his old guitar. He looks happy, energetic, and at the top of his form." Dylan put on a show that night that surely rivaled any he's ever done. He was not only smiling throughout the entire show, he was laughing. I couldn't remember the last time I saw Dylan laugh onstage. What a joy. The audience enjoyed Dylan, and Dylan enjoyed the audience.

After the show that Saturday evening, I went back to my hotel and fell into bed, exhausted. I awoke knowing I had to go to Greenwich Village and walk the streets that Bob Dylan walked when he was young and had his whole future ahead of him.

With some directions to "Dylan spots" in hand, I began my journey, though I hadn't planned on it actually being a *journey*. I was just going to kill time until the record shops opened at noon. I walked down Bleecker Street as the souvenir vendors began to put their wares out on the sidewalk. It was snowing lightly, which added a dark, melancholy feeling to the air. Suddenly, there was MacDougal Street, and I was captivated. It was fascinating to look at those old buildings and think of the countless young musicians who had walked in and out of their doors. I stumbled upon the Cafe Wha? and saw a notice on the side of the club that described its history. Of course, it mentioned Dylan. Then it was on to 116 MacDougal, where Dylan spent many hours at the old Gaslight Cafe. Just seeing the place made me shiver.

I noticed a cafe on the corner of Bleecker and MacDougal, so I stopped for something to eat. There I sat, sipping my coffee, knowing that in a few minutes I would get up, jump on a bus to the airport, and fly back to my hometown of Chicago. I didn't want to leave MacDougal Street, or Bleecker Street, or the Village, for that matter. I felt the ghosts of Dylan's past everywhere. I also felt the ghosts of my own past, and it made me sad. Bob Dylan was young when he walked those streets, and I was young once, too.

On the flight home, as dusk began blanketing the skies, I reflected on how Bob Dylan was such a large part of my life back then, and on how he affected who I am today. He made me think and he made me care, whether he wanted to or not. For this, I am eternally grateful.

My Bob Dylan weekend is over and I'm back home. The souvenirs have all been passed out to the kids. I told them of my adventure. My daughter understands, though I'm not sure my sons do, at least not yet. So, I sit at my laptop computer and type out these words to share with all those whose lives have been irrevocably altered by this man. Thank you, Bob.

1999

Series of Dreams

Dr. Andy Miller, *53, is a university lecturer and a practicing educational psychologist who lives in Matlock, Derbyshire, England. He has written and edited eight professionally relevant books and published a book of prose and poetry.*

Bournemouth Folk Club 1963, Royal Albert Hall 1966, the Isle of Wight 1969...I was there. Well, actually I wasn't, but I should have been.

Despite the intensity with which Bob Dylan's songs have been running around inside my head from the very beginning, I was compelled to avoid seeing the man live and in concert for many years. Now, some 36 years later, I've joined the ranks of specialist newsletter readership and the illicit concert CD collectors. I've rattled on the long overnight bus across Europe for three consecutive nights of gigs and contacted the Dylan telephone hotlines more often than my own family. Sad, perhaps, but this is recent. It was not always such.

My first acquaintance with Bob Dylan came when I was 17. There was a new guy in our school who had transferred in from elsewhere. Wealthy, he had access to a car and an air of studied coolness. But his attempts to ingratiate himself into our group left me cold. Somehow, though, in our provincial little English town, he seemed to have access to a wider knowledge of the world. One day, he pulled a record album from his school bag and asked if anyone would like a lift up the coast to see a concert at the Bournemouth folk club.

"This guy's really groovy, you've got to hear him," he said, in a vernacular that did not then feel entirely ludicrous.

I tried to imagine sharing the journey, the phony conversation, the ridiculous notion that any tastes of his could echo mine. I looked into the face on that first album cover, that baby face propped up by fear, sneer or whatever it was, and said, "I wouldn't go out of my way to see somebody who looks like that."

The second time I heard Dylan's name, the effect was also extreme, though in a very different way. Although British commercial television was still relatively new, the hour-long variety show, *Sunday Night at the London Palladium*, was already a national institution. The finale that particular evening was the current hot act, Peter, Paul & Mary. What little popular music was then televised I usually watched with my dad, who would criticize one group for its rhythm and another for the singer's diction. I secretly resented his opinions.

After the first song, and before a verdict was properly formed, Mary Travers stepped to the microphone and in solemn tones said something like, "There is a young man in America today writing songs that are touching the heart of a nation. His name is Bob Dylan, and this next song is called 'Blowin' in the Wind.'"

And my world changed. I was pulled across mountains and oceans by the emotion in the words and melody. In the silence afterwards, no judgment could be voiced. Everything had changed. I had been forced onto a new and unanticipated track, and there was no going back. Almost immediately, it dawned on me that I had thrown away the opportunity to see, and probably even meet, this young songwriter. That may have been the beginning of my reluctance to acknowledge the source of this much power as merely flesh and blood.

But I had a language now. Shortcutting home from school for lunch through the cemetery, I regaled my friend Rob: "It's like a conversation. He doesn't want a present, he just wants her to come back. When she says she isn't coming back, then he asks for these boots." But Dylan made the story overflow with cascading words and pictures: Oceans, diamonds, Western winds, stars. Boots of Spanish leather.

A year or so earlier, we'd hurried home at lunchtime through that same cemetery, fear strangling the conversation about Kennedy's ultimatum and the American blockade of Cuba. That morning, we had stood in the school assembly, the silence unbreakable, rigid and desperate for someone to take it all away. The same old hymns, the same old prayers, school football team results, netball teams, the Russian missile ships determined and straight on course, and those teachers unmasked, as impotent as us. And now we were trying to get back home in time to be together. My father would also be hurrying home from the bus stop, my mother in a steam-driven panic of preparation, my brother quiet in the living room. The clock ticking, the stages of nuclear alert, two minutes to midnight, all alone.

But at least I had a language: "Masters of War," "With God on Our Side," "When the Ship Comes In," "Only a Pawn in Their Game," "A Hard Rain's A-Gonna Fall."

Words in wave upon wave that could indeed drown out a whole world, make it clean, and lay strong, safe foundations.

Rob and I hitched through Europe in the summer of 1964, the first trip abroad for either of us. We started at the end of the seafront, right outside the back windows of Celia Wyatt's house. I had recovered from my tears on the beach and looked across at those net curtains, willing her to sit and wonder why, turn on her light and call out my name. A week or so later, I was standing in the red dust of a castle courtyard in Koblenz with each and every line from "Song to Woody" beating in around the fortress, from the sunset in the west, falling away down into the silver line of the Rhine far below. With the dust, in the wind. Born, gone. I had never been happier, nor more complete.

And, on occasion, I thought about my missed opportunity to see Dylan the year before. It would have been about half a crown to get into the folk club, about a quarter of my weekly paper-route earnings. I could have bought him an underage pint, struggled with tongue-tied conversation, and embarrassed us both by asking just how he was able to know my world inside-out. I didn't have to see any of the journalists mangled in those later interviews to know how very wrong it could have easily become. But it went deeper than that. Although I studied the early album covers, somehow I could still not believe that this was really just one human being at work. I bought the myth and loved the story, but I also doubted my sources. I couldn't imagine where all of this energy could originate, but it seemed impossible that it could be from within one young, slight human frame. I think it was feelings like this that were behind my never quite getting around to pursuing concert tickets and always managing to be temporarily distracted at precisely the wrong, or right, moment.

Midway through the '60s, I left for the city, first for casual work and then for college. Around me, around the world, sunspots erupted during those years, and the shadow extended its reach:

The vagabond, Louise, her lover, Dr. Filth, the agents, Jack the Ripper, Napoleon, Einstein, and T. S. Eliot.

John F. Kennedy. Dr. Martin Luther King, Jr. Prisoners and guards. Robert Kennedy. Weathermen and a wind blowing. Paris, Chicago, four dead at Kent State. Honesty outside the law. George Jackson cut down.

Something was still in the way, though. In 1966, I sat in my apartment (probably listening to *Another Side* or *Freewheelin'*) just a few miles away from Royal Albert Hall as Dylan plugged into the future. Judas in the flesh, taking silver.

I was selling deck chairs on Weymouth seafront in 1969, where I could almost see the Needles on the end of the Isle of Wight, as Dylan took the stage and proved that he had survived the motorcycle crash. Despite the long and eerie silence, he was whole and would occupy a physical, living presence before an audience.

Perhaps the film *Don't Look Back* would be a halfway house. After reading reviews about the savaging sarcasm Dylan inflicted on the unwary in the film, I kept away, fearful that the delicacy of so many of those early songs might disappear for good if I were to confront a reality that proved Dylan to be a downright nasty piece of work. I finally went to see it years later and came away lifted out of my young teacher's life, further captured by the aura around the man, struck by his patience and honesty in places and the delicious invention in those richly deserved savagings.

Things moved on, but the albums seemed to peter out. By 1970, after *New Morning*, I ceased expectations and retreated to the back catalog, reasonably happy with the idea that this would probably have to last. It seemed like plenty at the time. Then an old college friend stopped by in 1975 with a muffled tape, saying that it was much more like the early stuff. I tried to discern the words, skeptical that the former majesty could ever be repeated. It was hard to catch, something about revolution, cafes, and basements, and I was not persuaded.

But some months later, while sitting up uncharacteristically late given the exhausting schedule of my new baby's night feedings, Bob Harris played "Sara" on the *Old Grey Whistle Test*. And once more, that combination of language, music, and delivery sliced right back into those special nerve centers.

Things never really slipped back again after that. Before me was the greedy delight of filling in the missed albums from the previous years-*Pat Garrett and Billy the Kid, Planet Waves, Blood on the Tracks, Desire,* and *Hard Rain*. But something old and deep-rooted persisted, making it possible for me to pass on his 1978 appearances at Earl's Court and Blackbushe.

By 1980, he had done it again. He was back on the other side, upsetting everybody, regenerating all the anger and hostility, feeding off it, then putting it straight back into the music:

"Slow Train Coming," "When You Gonna Wake Up," "Gotta Serve Somebody," "Are You Ready," "Pressing On."

Feeling as unsettled, disconcerted, and let down as all the others, we sorted out the babysitters, arranged the travel, got the tickets, and went to Earl's Court in 1981. I was almost as curious about the audience as about the performer. Some were much older that I'd expected, while others were highly "respectable" in their appearance. There were even nuns a few rows ahead, the marijuana smoke wafting their way. There were the girl singers, and then the man himself, armed with new songs and issuing a brutal, direct challenge with overwhelming intensity. Some members of the audience reserved their cheers of recognition for the early songs, his older testament, as if rewarding him and trying to shape him up. And back came an even greater surge of energy, vehement like a prophet aware of the fast approaching reckoning. I could not begin to understand the man. I could see him and how small he looked and watch his body leaning into the songs. And though nothing detracted from the songs and all of their effects—the tenderness, the anger, the global, and the singularly personal—ultimately, nothing was revealed.

Life traveled on down the years, and when Dylan appeared in Britain more frequently in the late 1980s, I made up for the lost years. Some dozen or so concerts further on, I went to the British opening in Bournemouth in 1997, only months after the scare of Dylan's hospitalization. I drove down midweek in the heat of an Indian summer, taking leave from work on the first day of October. The sea pulsed a serious, inviting shade of indigo. The sand had been washed clean from the summer. And the beach, well, it was deserted except for...a distant figure coming toward me along the shoreline.

And I felt such a strong respect for the man. All those years along the sharp edge between art and celebrity, the heavy suffocation on the slight breath...surviving.

The figure moved closer, still just the two of us—35 years of words, tunes, and images. What if I blurted something out like those bewildered journalists back in 1965?

"Do you see yourself primarily as a poet or a folksinger?"

All the unexpected twists my life had taken, my friends, the loves, and the enmities. I wanted to tell him that this was the exact place where my children had played on the beach as babies. The arthritis in my knee stabbed as my foot skewed in the wet, rich sand. I could see the approaching figure bracing his back.

"Which comes first, the words or the music?"

The man, hunched, slight of build, probably mid-50s, came even closer, but I still could not see the face beneath the rage of curls.

"What is your latest protest?"

I stared at the sand, straining my peripheral vision as the figure passed right by me.

"Are you still religious?"

"How would you define folk rock?"

The next weekend, I went to Wembley with Jayne, my new partner. She warned me not to expect her to immerse herself in uncritical adulation (apparently some people do) and said that she liked some of Dylan's stuff. In fact, she really liked some of it, but said she couldn't stand that whining voice he sometimes used or that harmonica of his.

So many of the reviews of *Time Out of Mind* commented on the depression and despair running through the album. I'd played it a few times before the concert and formed the same impression. These were not just sad songs. This was the cry of a real sense of life slipping away, mortality standing square and solid up there in front on the track:

Some trains don't pull no gamblers,
No midnight ramblers like they did before,
I've been to sugar town, I shook the sugar down,
Now I'm tryin' to get to Heaven
Before they close the door.

And then I looked at him on that stage at Wembley, twisting the phrasing of those songs with new silences and rhythms, like brush strokes showing the picture as much in relief as in substance. Telling it. The old meanings reinvigorated and filling the hall, with extra nuances even now still springing out from the songs for the first time. Thinking it. Exaggerated postures, silly tilting of the head, arching eyebrows wringing out even more. Speaking it and breathing it. Big grins to the people in the front, seeming to say, "Hey, listen to this one. I like this bit. What do you think?"

Song building upon nonstop song, the pace never faltering and surprises around every corner. All of us dancing, rooted to the spot, right up close to the man on the stage. A glorious, unpredicted masterpiece was already fading as we stepped out into the night, and Jayne's verdict was, *"Brilliant."*

In fewer than nine months, he was back in England. We had taken around the best part of another year, a mild winter, a late spring, short holidays, work, and the daily round. Dylan, meanwhile, nearing 60 years old, had played 90 concerts, back and forth across the U.S., up and down the coasts, South America, Germany, Belgium, Holland, Sweden, Norway, and Ireland, keeping up the pace of the last 13 years. As if refreshed and energized by it all, once again he held the huge Sheffield arena in close to the moods of the music.

I stood between two of my sons, grown up as tall as me, while Dylan turned "The Times They Are A-Changin'" through his kaleidoscope. He had written this and so much more when only the age of my sons. But now there was more sadness, less angry demand in his call for parents to get out of the new road, not to criticize what they did not understand. And these over-familiar words chilled and transfixed me. For the very first time, I stopped hearing the song through my own young ears. I felt my sons pressed in close to me, but I could not turn to see their faces. I remembered the struggles with my own father. Were these two young men also out on their new road, beyond my command? Was I unwilling or unable to get out of the way or lend a hand?

It has finally occurred to me why I stopped avoiding Dylan's concerts. Once, I didn't want to be just another person burdening him with the responsibility of my appreciation, adding to that overwhelming stock of expectation heaped upon him. His angry assertions of the right to take the songs wherever he wanted, however, had shown time and again, decade after decade, hundreds after hundreds of songs, thousands after thousands of performances, that he really was immune to such pressures. I had also started out with that strange fear that the enormity of his work would somehow be diminished for me if I had living, breathing evidence that it really did originate in one man. Now, I realize that it has actually been the lesser albums and the occasional lackluster performances that have provided the salvation. Amongst all the sustained genius, for more than 35 years, is that human quality of variability. This is one human being at work, and the magnitude of his achievement is undiminished.

The Ultimate Bob Dylan Connection

BOB DYLAN MAGAZINE: In each issue you'll find several in-depth interviews with Dylan-related artists, a historical interview with Dylan himself, feature articles from world renowned writers, incredible previously unpublished photographs, and much more! Definitely not your usual fanzine–this high quality magazine was one of five finalists in the Music Journalism Awards along side *Rolling Stone, Mojo,* and *Entertainment Weekly. On the Tracks* is published 4 times per year including the *Annual Collector's Issue* at no extra charge.

BOB DYLAN NEWSLETTER: Keep up-to-date on the latest news articles compiled from around the world, concert information, set lists, latest releases, and more! *Series of Dreams* is published 12 times per year, and available only to *On the Tracks* subscribers.

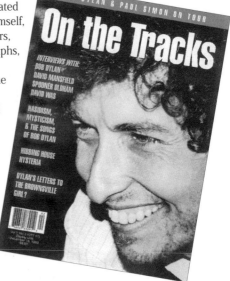

BOB DYLAN COLLECTIBLES: The *On the Tracks Annual Collector's Issue* offers the world's largest selection of Dylan merchandise with nearly two thousand new and out-of-print Dylan-related collectibles listed in each catalog! You'll find everything from books to t-shirts to ultra-rare collectibles.

BOB DYLAN CONCERT HOTLINE: *On the Tracks* subscribers have free access to *The Dylan Hotline*–updated weekly with upcoming concert information.

BOB DYLAN ON THE WEB: Our website (b-dylan.com) should be completed in early 2000. Watch for the announcement in *On the Tracks* or *Series of Dreams.*

On the Tracks magazine subscription costs $24.95 per year. The optional monthly newsletter, *Series of Dreams,* costs only $15.00 more. (Call or write for prices outside the U.S.) Send payment (Visa, Mastercard, personal check, or money order) to: Rolling Tomes Inc, PO Box 1943, Grand Junction, CO 81502 or call 970-245-4315 weekdays between 10 a.m. and 6 p.m. Mountain Time. 24-hour fax: 970-243-8025. E-mail: orders@b-dylan.com. Subscribe today!

Have *you* had a personal encounter with Bob?

Want to tell us about it? We've enjoyed collecting these stories, and will continue to do so. This book represents only 50 of the thousands of fans who must have had a personal encounter with Bob Dylan over his long career. If you have a story you might like to see published some day, e-mail it to Bob@humblepress.com, or snail-mail it to humble press.

Want another copy of this book?

Telephone orders:
Call toll free 1(800) 306-7168. We are open Monday through Friday from 9 A.M. to 6 P.M. Pacific time. Visa, Mastercard, or American Express card accepted.

Fax orders: (415) 333-9351

Postal orders: humble press, P.O. Box 4322, Daly City, CA 94016-4322

Online orders: order@humblepress.com

Web site: http://www.humblepress.com

Please send _____ copies of *Encounters with Bob Dylan* at $15.95 each.
I understand that I may return any books for a full refund if I am not satisfied.

Name: _____

Address: _____

City: _____ State: _____ Zip:_____

Sales Tax: Please add 8.25% ($1.32 each) for books shipped to California addresses.
U.S. Priority Mail (2-3 days): $3.50 for up to three books to same address.
Book rate (3-4 weeks): $2.00 for first book and 75 cents for each additional book.
Payment: Checks and Visa, Mastercard, and American Express accepted. Please include credit card number, expiration date, and the exact name on card.

Call 1(800) 306-7168 toll free, and order now